YOUR INNER JOURNEY TO

JANINE DUTHAC

Your Inner Journey to the Real

—

Finding your True Self and the art of joyful relating

Index compiled by Mary Kirkness

Illustrations by the author

SAFFRON WALDEN
THE C.W. DANIEL COMPANY LIMITED

First published in Great Britain in 1998
by The C. W. Daniel Company Limited
1 Church Path, Saffron Walden, Essex, CB10 1JP, United Kingdom

© Janine Duthac, 1998

ISBN 0 85207 319 4

Produced in association with Book Production Consultants plc
25–27 High Street, Chesterton, Cambridge, CB4 1ND, UK
Designed & typeset by Ward Partnership, Saffron Walden, Essex
Printed in England by Hillman Printers (Frome) Ltd, Frome, Somerset

*This book is dedicated with love
and gratitude to the One Glorious Life*

CONTENTS

FOREWORD

This is a remarkable book.

Here, at last, is a clear and unpretentious guide to the true purpose of life and the real identity of every human being. Distilled from actual lived experience it is extremely practical. At the same time you also cannot fail to become aware that this knowledge originates from a level of mind beyond that of even the most sophisticated intellect. Each sentence has a depth of meaning which will often compel you to stop reading in order to have time to reflect on its content.

What makes this book unique and stand above the rest is that here, for the *first time ever* to my knowledge, we are given a precise, simple diagnosis of the *real root cause* of all of humanity's problems. It spells out how these arise and, as a result, how to become free from the "prisons" in which most of us find ourselves. In so doing we learn how to sort out our relationships with ourselves and others.

The writing in this book is charged with a dynamic energy and real optimism which will uplift you and fill you with enthusiasm to take charge of your life!

As we head towards the millennium which many view as the end of one age and the beginning of a new age, the timing and timeliness of this book could not be better.

Gordon Sherry (PhD)
Johannesburg, South Africa
August 1997

CHAPTER I

THE INNER JOURNEY

The inner journey is the way back Home, to your Source, to the kingdom of Heaven, your origin, the truth and your true self.

This journey is one of the most thrilling and exacting adventures you are likely to accomplish. It is full of tests and trials, failures and victories, dragons and snares to overcome, tears and pain, laughter and moments of joy.

Nobody can take this journey for you and do not think that you can have a free ride on someone else's back. Nobody can eat and sleep for you, or walk for you. **You** have to take your own journey Home. When **you** feel ready you will naturally decide to go Home.

You need to begin with an intention to find your Self, or the Truth, or what Life is really all about. If your intention is not a true or sincere one you **will** not find your way Home. If you do not intend to find your way Home you **will** not get There. Without an intention there is no direction, no focus. Once you have the vision – to go Home – and the intention to do so you also need to make a commitment, an agreement with yourself, to find the way to the Truth, Home.

You have the perfect guide within you – Life or God within. Life-God knows all, knows the way and knows you perfectly. You will not find the way in books as it has to be experienced. It is not a conceptualized theory or an intellectual game. Neither is it a belief system or an act. It is a happening, something that is happening to you and that you live in every day life.

The way Home is to the centre of yourself. A symbol for your whole self is a circle. This is made up of "layers" or aspects of yourself through which you are going to explore. At the same time you are journeying through certain aspects of Life, or levels of Life that you are becoming aware of.

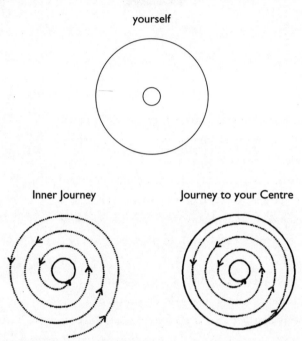

There are seven levels of Life. The first level is essential Life, which is divine. The second level is the level on which your spirit, a spark of Life, existence or being, exists. Another one of your higher bodies is on the third level. Your soul, your causal body, is on the fourth level. On this level is your intuition – that with which we directly know. The mental body is on the fifth level, the emotional body on the sixth level and the etheric and physical bodies are on the seventh level. Your mental, emotional, etheric and physical bodies make up your personality, the form aspect of Life. The form aspect, or Mother, is the Creation.

The spirit, the Father aspect, permeates the form, the Mother aspect, and out of their union a soul, or Son/Daughter (a child), is born. Here we have the Trinity. The spirit is in the formless world, the kingdom of God or Heaven, and the personality lives in the form world, in God's

Creation, paradise or the Garden of Eden. The soul links the two worlds.

The journey back to Source, to Heaven, where all of Creation comes from, begins on the densest level of Life – the seventh level – and continues to the sixth, fifth, fourth and so on. There are no short cuts. Each level has to be completely explored. Each level is more subtle than the last, so the lessons along the way get more and more difficult and we are required to become more and more sensitive in order to register what is going on.

To get back to the Kingdom of Heaven we have to journey through matter, the form aspect. It is like climbing up a mountain, the mountain of matter (Mater), so that one can arrive at the formless world of Heaven, the Father's House. A triangle or a cone can be used to symbolize the mountain of matter:—

The mountain of Matter

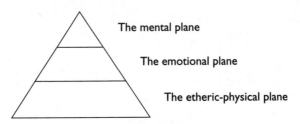

The mental plane

The emotional plane

The etheric-physical plane

Journey up the mountain of Matter

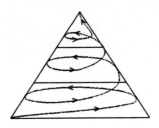

While we are adventuring through the levels of Life we are discovering what our bodies are made up of and learning to tame – master – them so that they do not run away with us, until eventually we have tamed our

entire personality and are ready then to move onto soul level. We are also learning about Life through Life experience. As we find out how Life does and doesn't work, step by step, we expand our conscious awareness and replace our ignorance with conscious knowledge about Life or the truth. The truth is the Light. We eventually become fully enlightened.

The first step is to get in touch with yourself and find out where you are at. You will sense the areas that you need to work on. You need to find out consciously what you are made up of and your true identity. That is why you need to get in touch with what you are **feeling** here and now. If you **think** of how you think you "should be" you will be caught in a theory, which will prevent you from discovering where you are at actually, in consciousness. When you start the inner work the quest begins. Aim true and you will head for the Light.

Beyond the personality is the soul, the intuition. The moment we reach beyond the intellect, beyond matter, we intuitively register and know that we are aspects of the One Life. We get to know our Selves for the first time, we are at-one with the One Life, the Glory, and find that we are home. Home is the One Life, omnipresent, here and now. Consciously knowing, at last, that you are "That" – an aspect of the One Life, the Glory – brings joy, happiness and exuberance.

The moment that you have transcended matter, in conscious aware-ness, is the moment that you have come Home. This is where many fairy stories come to the end. This is when Heaven and Earth in you – your spirit and your personality – meet, when your higher mind and your lower mater-ial mind and all aspects of yourself come together and unite, i.e. get married in the fairy story symbolism. It is when the dragon has been slain or when the witch's spell has been dispelled and the witch has disappeared, the brambles have been cut through with the sword of discernment and you are no longer lost in the forest of delusion. The battle of Arjuna (see the Indian scripture *The Bhagavad Gita*) is won, Cinderella has finished sweeping up (all the nonsense and bad habits on the three levels of Mater), the stone statues come back to Life, the princess wakes up, the seven chakras, or dwarfs, are aligned and Snow White has become purified, the sun-Light – the Son – comes out and the darkness vanishes, Prometheus is unbound, the prisoner is set free and you live "happily ever after" in the Father's House – the Heaven world.

The Son, the soul – the Christ child or Buddha nature – symbolized by the white (purified) unicorn, is born.

The end is the beginning of another adventure in the Heaven World and the story continues . . .

RELATIONSHIP WITH YOURSELF

What you essentially are is a perfectly beautiful whole and complete unit of Life created by God, because you are an aspect of the One Glorious Life. Symbolically you are the prince or princess in the fairy stories, or a child of Life.

That you have life is the greatest and most wonderful gift that you can ever have. Cherish this gift and do not take it for granted. **You** have to make your life worthwhile. Nobody else can do this for you. Now is the only opportunity you have to get on with it. Encourage yourself and set yourself up to cope with whatever Life presents to you.

You need to get to know yourself. You are the one that you have to work with, the one that you have to bring Up in conscious awareness. Observe what you are doing and what is going on. Watch and study all your actions, reactions, thoughts and motives.

We are all ignorant and have come to school on Earth to learn about Life consciously. You can trust yourself to find your way through. You can trust Life, your senses, your instinct, your intellect and intuition. God within you guides you perfectly, so learn to listen.

Everything you need is inside of yourself. You can find attributes within yourself that you can nurture and grow. You do not have to attach yourself to others and demand that they give you the things that you are "lacking".

Our conscious awareness of Life and relating is not complete and is therefore "faulty". We make big mistakes in our approach to ourselves,

Life and others. We need to admit these mistakes, learn from them and rectify them. In finding the solutions to these problems we find the light of reality, and get rid of the flaws in our conscious awareness.

Love yourself. If you do not love yourself you will not endure the journey Home, or be able to heal and free yourself and succeed. You need to learn to love yourself unconditionally. The more you judge yourself the more prison walls you build around yourself and the more miserable you make yourself. Judging your mistakes doesn't help you to overcome them. When you love yourself and take 100 per cent responsibility for yourself you can liberate yourself. Nobody else can save you from the mistaken choices that you have made.

With love comes respect and consideration. You need to respect yourself and have consideration for yourself. If you have no self respect the clumsy will tread all over you and the selfish will use and abuse you. Without self respect you have no chance and you will not treat yourself well, which will be depressing. If you have no self respect how are you going to take responsibility for yourself? If you neglect or turn away from yourself you will not stand a chance. If you avoid yourself and your life you will feel insecure.

Be honest with yourself. **The Truth liberates you.** Without the Truth you cannot find your way Home.

Be true to "yourself". If you are not true to "yourself" you will get into a mess. If you are true to "yourself", reality, then you are true to all else – Life. If you deceive yourself you will lead yourself astray and will at some stage have to unravel this tangle. Deception is a quagmire. When you deceive yourself you give yourself a very hard life, in hell. When you are true to "yourself" you naturally do it right.

You need to develop, expand and stretch yourself through your talents. For this you need a great deal of experience. Give yourself the opportunity to experience what you need.

You came into incarnation with a purpose. You need to carry it out. Do not allow others to impose their ideas onto you about what they think you "should be" doing (to please them). You have the right to fulfil your purpose.

Put yourself **first** in an unselfish way, then you can take responsibility for yourself, your life. You are **as** important as others, not more important or less important than they are. Put yourself last and you will come last – you will not get anywhere.

You have a life to get on with and it is not selfish to do so. It is the only one that you can get on with and only you can get on with it. Nobody else can and you do not have to wait for anyone else to tell you what to do with your life. This is entirely your choice. Your life is your responsibility. Your life is what you make of it with your free choice. What are you waiting for? Give yourself the permission to get on with it. You decide what happens to you. If you allow others to dictate to you, you will not be free, free to create your own life.

If you don't take responsibility for your life you cannot get on with it. Only you can take responsibility for your life. If you are expecting someone else to get on with your life for you, you are going to wait for a long, long time . . . If you do not get on with it you are letting yourself and all of Life down. You also need to learn to get on with yourself because you are with yourself always. You cannot free yourself unless you are self reliant. There is no escape from yourself.

Allow yourself to be you. It is a great relief to allow yourself to be just as you are, i.e. without judgement. You cannot be anyone else but yourself so don't try. You don't have to do anything to be you. You are already you. You cannot rehearse being you. To be yourself you do not need an image or an act. **You** are not an act, although you have the ability to act a part. Being your true self is a joy and is effortless. You simply are. What you are is what you are. You cannot really be anything else but what you really are.

You can pretend all sorts of things and wear hundreds of masks but these acts, if you identify with them, imprison you too. Being is fun. Not allowing yourself to be you is a painful, joyless experience.

Allow yourself to be exactly where you are at and bring yourself up from there. What is the point of pretending to be somewhere else in some kind of act or fantasy? And do not push yourself to grow. You can grow Up naturally.

Accept yourself and where you are at and the situation that you are in. Then you can work from there. If you resist yourself – actually what you are doing – and the situation you are in, it will get you down and you will not be able to cope with it. If you cannot accept where you are at you cannot move on in conscious awareness.

If you play useless games with yourself, for example, the "I can't" game, you will not get anywhere. "I can't" is a terribly limiting and depressing game to play with yourself, and it is an excuse. There are much better games to play, for example, "I **can** find my way through," which gives you the permission to get on with it and to reach out into the limitless.

Self-pity doesn't work. It is an indulgence and it doesn't help. You need to learn to help yourself. If you help yourself you can succeed and if you succeed how can you feel sorry for yourself?

If you think that you do not count or that you are worthless, no good, you put yourself **down**, upset yourself and let yourself and Life down. How can you enjoy yourself if you believe that you are worthless? If you condemn yourself as "bad" that is all that you are allowing yourself to act out – a bad person – and you are stuck with this act until you change it.

If you do not value yourself and your life you will abuse yourself. Cheap values bring no happiness and satisfaction. Invest your energies in cheap values and you will reap cheap returns. Invest your time and energy in quality and simplicity and you will live an uncluttered life of quality.

You need to bring yourself **Up**, up into the Light. To do this you need to learn to be your own best friend. If you are not on your side, Life's side, you will not get anywhere. You need to care for yourself and take care of yourself. If you are not on your side then you are against yourself and in that case you do not care about yourself.

What you idealistically think you "should **be**" is a concept that ends up being an act. "I should be more loving," becomes an act of a loving person. You need to tune into what **is** happening inside and work with that. When you try to fit yourself into a "should be" you are squeezing yourself into one of your own thoughtforms (ideas) which becomes another prison wall.

You are not what you think you are. What you think you are is a concept. You are not a concept of yourself. You cannot conceptualize being. Being is beyond thought. **You** were there **before** you had any ideas about yourself. What you really are is not a concept of what you really are. Being is beyond acts. You cannot act being.

You **can** only work with what **is** going on inside of yourself. What you think you "should be" is a fiction, and attempting to impose a fiction onto what is, is not worthwhile. Being yourself is much more fun than trying to be some cumbersome act.

What you **are** and what you are **doing** are two different things. You cannot change what you are – a unique aspect of the One Life. You can change what you are doing, the way that you are behaving, your manners and conduct. Aim to be completely harmless in all your actions.

If you expect too much of yourself, or have any other unrealistic ideas that you are trying to achieve, you will not only make yourself unhappy, you may break down or kill your personality trying to accomplish the impossible.

You are an aspect of "Life Divine". This is nothing to hide and be ashamed of. Happiness and joy come from your relationship with your true self and Life. Only you can get this relationship together. Playfulness is the expression of joy.

At the centre of yourself you find your self, "Life Divine". This is when you come Home to omnipresent Life and the God that gave you life.

CREATING YOUR LIFE

Man has been given the power to create and work with energies. You have been made by God to be a creator, a magician, with a free choice. Within certain parameters you can create what you choose with your life. Eventually we need to learn to be conscious creators.

You do need to have a vision for your life, otherwise you will do nothing with it and your life will seem to have no purpose. A creator has a dream, or vision, to actualize.

You are a living being full of energy, which can be expressed constructively in a creative way, destructively or neutrally. You have to choose in what manner you express yourself. The creative ideas that we have are beneficial and uplifting. These then are white magic. The ugly ideas that we spell out, in words, become the wicked spells in the fairy stories, are a destructive force and are a mis-use of our creative abilities. They are black magic.

If you choose to be a white magician then you will practise harmlessness. As we spell things out, in word forms, it is necessary to be harmless in our speech too.

Earth is a school of learning, a play school, a stage. You decide what role you are going to play out, for example doctor, artist, engineer, musician, scientist. You decide how you are going to play this out and how you are going to behave, i.e. you write the script. It is all up to you.

What you decide is acceptable conduct for you is what you act out and do. You are making up the rules for your individual world. You are the ruler of your individual world, or your life. With a wave of a magic "wand" you can change the rules, your role and the script. Because you have this ability you are also the author of your destiny and karma.

Who has the **say** – (sounded out created thoughtforms) – or authority, in your life? **Who** is creating your life? You? Others? Other egos? Who is in charge of your life? You do not have to allow other people – creators – to impose their created thoughtforms, their will, onto you and your world.

The world that you create for yourself is made up of thoughtforms that you said were in order. These ideas and beliefs, that make up our individual worlds, may be true or false. You spelled out these decrees – ideas or rules – for yourself. You can change these rules whenever you like. They are not fixed, hard and fast, unless you create them this way.

If you have made hard and fast rules and fixed points of view then you cannot be flexible and fluid. You will be inflexible and intolerant, for example a fanatic, and you will be unable to flow with Life.

This world of yours is your "frame of mind". How you respond to Life and others depends on your frame of mind.

The final conclusions you come to about aspects of Life become the world you made. For example:–

Winter **is** depressing. Carrots **are** good for you. Women **are** not to be trusted. All doctors know what they are doing. The Earth **is** flat. God is in the clouds. Boiled onions **are** disgusting. Only my church **is** right. My country **is** the best. I hate Communists, etc. Having decided these

things you will always find winter depressing, you will be happy to eat carrots, you'll probably avoid women, trust all doctors, think people who say that the Earth is round are insane, look for God in the clouds, start retching when you smell boiled onions, snub all other churches that are not the same as yours, feel superior to all nationalities that are not yours and condemn all Communists.

When you say things to yourself you are informing yourself of how life **is**. If the ideas are true ones then you have well informed yourself. If they are untrue ideas you have misinformed yourself with nonsense.

You have a choice. You can build your world with truths, realities, i.e. related to reality, that you have verified for yourself, through Life experience, or with illusions, nonsense, i.e. what is not true and therefore false. Illusions make up our hells and the hell experience and cause untold suffering. You do not have to be trapped in the forms of your magic. You can create whatever you wish.

Your world is the way you create your life. Your life does not have to be a boring, dreary, depressing, distressing, hell experience. You are the script writer. **You** say what you can experience. When you take charge of your mind and take charge of your world you can re-create it – change your limiting mindsets, throw out illusions for truths, heal your life and yourself.

You do not have to wait for something to happen or for someone to come along and make it happen for you. You cannot expect someone else to get rid of the spells around you, to give you permission to do what you want to do, etc. **You** have to do this for yourself.

We express ourselves via our thoughtforms about ourselves. If we have negative ideas about ourselves "I am inferior/a reject/useless," for example, then our behaviour will be negative, destructive, because this is how we have created ourselves. These ideas about ourselves make us miserable, if not suicidal.

Life-negating ideas make your world a grim and ugly nightmare. This is unnecessary, unless you intend to suffer.

A negative instruction to the mind is not an instruction, for example, "I'll never marry a Virgo/an artist/a Brit." It does not say who you can marry. The mind has got "marry a" and "Virgo/artist/Brit", so it manifests that. This is why people say "Never say 'never'."

When you change the original ideas in your mind you change your frame of mind. When you do this you change your vibrations and attract something else into your life. This is how to change your life. You do it from within; not without. You may change the country you live in, but if you haven't changed your mindsets you will attract to yourself the same experiences. You have to change the fundamental ideas in your mind.

You only get to change the things that **you see** are not working for you. You can only change your vibrations once you have seen and understood clearly what you need to work on and do it.

If you create nothing with your life, then that is what will happen – nothing.

You do not have to be the victim of any thoughtforms. You can drop and discard the ones that you don't want – yours and the ideas of others, but you can only do this if you take responsibility for your life and your world. You **say** what experiences you can and can't have. You have to clean up your world and free yourself.

When others break the rules we have made for our own worlds we usually get angry and shocked. "How dare you do that!". They have their own rules and ideas of lawlessness.

You can construct useful thoughtforms and you can destroy, or dispel, thoughtforms that you do not need. Let your thoughtforms work for you.

As we gradually grow in conscious awareness, the world, the life we are creating, expands and changes; as our values change so does our world. The world, or life, we create for ourselves reflects our state of conscious awareness.

When you re-create your world, and save yourself from nonsense, you need to employ sound, healthy, truthful, realistic ideas. We need to dis-spell insane illusions with the Truth.

You need to bring up your world of conscious awareness into the Light of the Truth.

You have the power to create a perfectly happy, beautiful life for yourself, providing you are true to Life, your true self and if you give up playing silly, harmful games with yourself and other people. You can get your life back to its inherent perfect state by giving up nonsense.

ACTS AND GAMES

Life on Earth is a play School, a stage. We are the creators that choose what roles we play out, the scripts and if we want to continue playing the games, or role parts, we are acting out.

Before we incarnated each of us chose our parents, culture and country for a purpose. This role we play out for a whole lifetime. For example, you chose to "be" (play out actually) the daughter of Presbyterian parents, who are farming in Scotland, and who have three sons. You therefore are playing the role of sister to three males.

How you respond to "your" parents and brothers, Scotland, the language, the Presbyterian church, farming, haggis, kilts, bagpipes, Scottish dancing, etc is entirely your choice. This scenario that you have chosen for yourself is unavoidable. You cannot change your sex, or the height of your physical body, pretend that you are a Chinaman, that you have three sisters, and that your parents are doctors.

You may, when you have grown up, decide to leave Scotland, drop the church, not speak to your parents and brothers again, but this does not alter the upbringing that you have had or the colour of your hair.

What you do with your life is your choice. This is your creation. You may choose to "be" – act out – a ballet dancer, let us say, marry later in life, birth ten children and "become" a choreographer when you can no longer dance. Here we have the roles you have chosen to play out in your life – dancer, wife, mother, choreographer. These are the obvious roles or games. Children practice playing out these sorts of career games.

There are more subtle games that we play out with ourselves and others, for example the martyr, the romantic, the idealist.

On an even more subtle level there are hundreds of other make-believe games that we dream up and play out, act, such as:–

I am such a spiritual person. I am so serious. I am a tough guy. I haven't got time. I am wise. I am the strongest. I can't. Life is hard. Poor me. I'm the king of the castle, and you are the dirty rascal. I am not good enough. Reject me. I am such a good little server. Nothing I do is good enough. Sure I'll play your victim. I am a delicate female. I am a dumb blonde. I am only little. I am so enlightened. I know it all. I am such a good parent. I am so sexy. I am so wonderful.

How can you act "being spiritual" when you are a spirit? How can you act "being sexy" when your physical body has been created to be sexual? You are **naturally** wonderful, dignified and sexy.

The characters or images that we choose to play out can be terribly limiting. For example, "I am a Scottish Presbyterian. I therefore hate the British, and I can be rude to Catholics and Anglicans and ignore all other faiths and nationalities." This means that you have cut yourself off from the rest of humanity, when humanity is, in reality, one family. Of what earthly use is this? We, humanity, are on this planet together and we have to share this world, because we **are** sharing this world.

Other people, who are irresponsible users, cunningly set us up to play extremely negative roles without us being aware of what is happening. For example, you have a drunk mother who is "motherless". She has to be parented, taken care of. She is too drunk to drive home so you have to drive her home, etc, etc, etc, etc. Over the years she trains you to "become" (act out) a caretaker of the irresponsible. You do not realize this. The role has become an inbuilt habit, so years later you are still looking for other "helpless" persons to take care of.

You do not **have** "to be" (act out) any roles that other people desire you to play for them. Their concepts of what you "should be", for them, imprison you.

Are you playing worthwhile, uplifting games and roles, or are you dragging yourself, humanity and the planet down with destructive, joyless games? If so why and for what purpose?

Watch your behaviour most carefully and you will see what roles you are playing out. You can change your habitual roles any time you choose to. Once you have established what roles you are not going to carry on playing, then you need a vision of what you are going to play out.

Nobody can quit playing a game, a part, for you. A psychologist cannot give up a part for you. You have to choose to quit the game.

Behind all the myriad roles and masks that you have is you, the actor. **You are not your act.** If you act the role of Oberon in the play *A Midsummer Night's Dream*, that does not mean that you **are** Oberon. When you go back stage and take off the costume **you** are still there.

If you identify with your acts and the roles you play out you will be imprisoned by them and you will not be able to play your true self, a joyful, playful child of Life. Then you will lose sight of your Self and get lost in the dark. You will be playing out painful illusions, because you **are not** your acts. Your masks prevent you from enjoying and expressing your Self. You cannot act your Self. You can only be your Self. Playing your Self, a child of Life, is effortless, a joy.

When you believe that you are your act, or acts, then you are split between your act and your real Self.

Living up to an image you have in mind of your "Self", and fooling yourself with it, prevents you from being honest with yourself, being true to your real self about yourself and from getting in touch with who you really are. You live in a fantasy, not in the real world.

Of course you can wholeheartedly put yourself into an act, but when you identify with it you get stuck in an illusion, a painful prison. An act is a concept of a role to play out, and is therefore an illusionary "self". If you try to play out any form of illusion and **be** the part, you have unwittingly gone against your real self. The verbs "to be" and "to act" are not the same verb.

It is in order to make-believe a part and play it out, providing it is useful and that you know that it is an act and that you are not fooling anyone, including yourself, with it. You can act whatever you like. The question, "Who are you?" remains.

Our fixed ideas about ourselves keep us stuck in the same roles. When you give up play-acting set, make believe parts, you can play anything because you are free and flexible.

When you express yourself through a nasty thoughtform, or character, your energies are distorted into ugly, destructive act-ions. Obviously this will not give you any happiness.

Your acts prevent others from relating to you. The person cannot relate to you because the acts, the illusions, stand in the way. If you insist on playing Oberon every day you are putting people into the position of having to relate to Oberon, not you.

Our acts create barriers between us. Behind all acts is simply a human being.

Your acts prevent you from relating to Life and to others. The acts you have identified with remove you from reality. Who do you think you are fooling with your acts?

The more you try to "be", for example, good and loving the more you are removed from being your real self. You have trapped and imprisoned your real self in concepts of how you think you "should be", i.e. in acts. You can act anything at all except your real self. You are beyond concepts of your real self. **The real you is naturally loving and beautiful**, so it is not necessary to act a loving person. You are not a concept, a pretence, an illusion. You are the real. Why not be in the real world playing your real self in Light?

You do not have to do anything to be, because you already **are**. You do not have to get dressed up into some kind of part and costume in order to be your real self. To find your real self you have to take off all the masks and the costumes. When you let your real self be, you have no poses, no masks, no props and no scripts. You do not play out make-believe "you's".

Because people think that they **are** their acts they take them very, very seriously. Most of our acts are a ridiculous farce. When we finally see through our own acts, and how absurd they are, we end up laughing at ourselves. What we were doing was playing the fool, in numerous guises, because we fooled ourselves into thinking that we **are** our acts and that they were all so important.

If you take other people's acts seriously you are deluded.

The **best** you can be is your real self. Acts veil the Light within you. Why hide That? You can be you without pretences, images and other illusions. Being present here and now is not a concept. Practising a concept becomes an act. Allowing your real self to be means getting rid of your concepts of yourself and your acts. Being is not something that you solve in your mind. It is beyond your mind. Being is something that you experience, celebrate.

When we "die" and go back stage, Home for the School holidays, we stop playing out all our roles, such as the Scottish lass that became the ballet dancer, etc. There is no death. We go back stage for a while and return to play out another part in this School of experiential Education.

HOME-CONDITIONING

Our parents represent the male and female principles in Life and the Father and Mother aspects in Creation.

If you have, for example, a wonderful father and a difficult mother you may conclude, unconsciously, that all men are wonderful and feel comfortable with the Father aspect, and that all women are difficult and have difficulties coming to terms with the Mother aspect and mothering. You will probably get on well with men and not relate to women successfully.

The way our parents treat us is the way we unconsciously believe we deserve to be treated by ourselves and others. If our parents treat us with respect we will go out into Life with self respect and expect others to respect us. If we are abused by our parents we do not expect others to respect us, and may even consider those who are kind and considerate towards us as being somewhat insane.

Our parents demonstrate to us how to relate and behave. Your father may hit your mother, so you learn that the way men are supposed to relate to women is to hit them now and again, even if you do not like what is being done. If you are the daughter you will unconsciously find a husband who hits you. If you are the son you will hit your wife. If you are consciously aware that this is not nice, that you can relate in other ways and conjure up other possibilities, you have then discarded this aspect of your upbringing training and will not play it out.

Home-conditioning is a training in relating, which we play out later on in Life, mainly unconsciously. During our upbringing our roles and ways of relating are established. If you want to change these mindsets, the way your parents moulded your consciousness, you have to wake up to what is going on and change them consciously.

We carry many mindsets from our upbringing – family, cultural, religious, national. Your mindsets turn out to be your scripts and scenarios in Life. Any fixed ideas that you may have about yourself, positive or negative, have accompanying roles to play out. These need to be carefully looked into and discarded if they are unfair and destructive.

You can wipe out your negative home-conditioning mindsets and make a new life for yourself.

Negative home-conditioning mindsets wreck your life. The, "I am a reject," "I am worthless," "I am a failure," "I am a psychological rubbish-bin," and other victim roles that parents have taught their children to play, are the hell experience. It is not surprising that the people who get trapped in these roles feel suicidal. **You do not have to play out these Life-negating roles.** You can give up unhealthy, unhappy ways of relating. You do not have to play out nasty home-conditioning mind-sets for ever!

Some churches have misled us into believing that we **are** miserable sinners, in other words that we **are** intrinsically bad, which is highly destructive nonsense. What God Created is beautiful, not bad. What we have created for ourselves out of ignorance, with our own free choice, may be detrimental, but we can rectify our wrong doings. If we are intrinsically bad then there is no hope for us, no liberation, no salvation.

The only reason why we have any mindsets from our upbringing, in the first place, is because our parents and other adults are the author-ities in our lives. We have to undo and unlearn all the illusions and Life negation roles and games they taught us to play.

Parents demonstrate to their children, "This is your lot in this life. This is all that you deserve." Your life does not have to be the way your parents and other authorities, in your upbringing, created it. It can be the way you create it.

AUTHORITIES

While we are growing up we have numerous authorities – parents, grandparents, aunts and uncles, elder brothers and sisters, teachers at school, priests, doctors and dentists, etc. We came to learn and so we are open to receive knowledge and guidance from those who we think know. We do need parenting and guidance.

We take what our authorities say as the truth, so we take them seriously. Even when they talk nonsense we take them seriously. Non-sense taken seriously causes much pain.

We have been trained to respect and obey our elders and the authorities without question. When we are children we do not have the power, authority, to say, "No," to the awful things that are being done to us. We are not taught to be free thinkers or to be true to ourselves. They have fed into our minds thousands of ideas, true or false, that have shaped our lives and our worlds. In order to free ourselves we need to go through the collective hell of humanity's illusions, which we have contributed to in past lives. It is up to us to toothcomb through this pile of trash and weed out the nonsense that we have been told. We do not have to give up truthful ideas. This can take many years of inner work.

People who do not yet think for themselves find authorities, or leaders, to follow. Any authority plays a parent role for you, which means that you are not taking full responsibility for yourself.

It is when we begin to think for ourselves that we start to question our authorities and have the opportunity to find out what Life is really all about. Once you have given up human authorities you have a free mind to enquire with, question – quest – with. Then there is only one authority left to turn to – your real self, God within.

If you take charge of your life and yourself then **you** can authorize, or allow, what happens to you and what roles you choose to play out. If you rely on anyone else, i.e. have no self-reliance, you are not free. You are waiting for someone to tell you what to do.

As soon as you make someone, or a group of people, your authority and obey the person, or group, you have lost the authority, power over yourself. You have given your power away. You have to wait for them to give you the permission to do things and are open to their auto-suggestions. You have given them the **say** in your life so they can spell out what you do. If you conform without questioning anything you will not be free to find the truth for yourself.

There is only one true authority on this Creation and that is God, our Planetary Logos, as God created It. No human is the authority on this Creation. **Let God, Life, within you be your only authority. Let God within you come first in your life, above everyone else.** God Knows all and knows you perfectly. Nobody else does. Our human gods and idols out there may know some things, but they are all ignorant. So are you. If you let the ignorant guide you, you are going to be misled.

If you put anything before God within, Life, then you block God and Life Itself out, and dis-connect yourself from your Source. Nothing and nobody is **more** important than God, Life, within.

Some people do set themselves up to be a god, an authority. Religious gods say, "Without me you will not get to Heaven." They stand directly in your way of listening to God within, and being guided back home to Heaven. These fools are implying that they know it all, when they do not, that God within can't guide you home and that this School of Life doesn't work, which is ridiculous.

Are you listening to the instructions of the priest, for example, or are you listening to the inner voice and being true to that? Listen within to find out if someone is talking nonsense or not. Is what they are saying ringing true or not?

The masters know much. Even so do not put them before God within you. There is only one true authority in Life and that is God within.

The rules of any religious form of worship, or mode of conduct in society, were made to assist humanity. You do not have to sacrifice your real self, God within, for these rules.

You cannot listen to God within, be true to that and then obey some controller or dictator, who is more than likely ordering you to do something contrary to your guidance. Trying to listen within and without, at the same time, causes inner conflict.

Putting some aspect of Life before Life means that you have created something or someone as more important than the whole of Life Itself, which is nonsense. Out of the One essential Life came all the millions of aspects of Life.

We sacrifice our lives to the idols we created. This is a useless sacrifice.

Do not put anybody before God within you. If you do you will veil out the light within. **There is One Life, one power, one glory. Let God guide you through your life.**

GUIDANCE

We are being guided all the time by our loving God and our guides (masters), whether we are aware of it or not.

Humanity has basically three approaches to God – God up there separated from us; no God, which usually means the person is stuck in his or her intellect and is not seeing the whole; and those who have at-oned with Life and know that we are not separated from God, Life.

If you are emotionally focused and are only starting to think for yourself a sure way of guidance is to ask yourself, (actually your true self), whatever specific thing you have in mind. Listen deep within, beyond your fears and desires, to what you **feel** about it. What you feel, with your innermost feelings, will obviously not be verbal. What you think may very well be faulty, because one does not always have all the facts to think with.

Guidance comes from beyond mind and may not always seem to be reasonable. Go where you feel drawn.

You can always ask God for guidance at any time. The answer can come in numerous ways, so you need to be watchful and to listen carefully with your inner ear. Someone may tell you exactly what you need to hear; you may open a book at the right page; the message may come in a dream or some other way. We are given wonderful guidance in dreams.

The advice dreams that we have come in symbolic forms and are tailor-made for us, according to our own individual mythology. A bicycle, for example, will mean something different to each person. It is necessary to ask yourself what the symbols mean to you, in order to understand your dreams. There are certain symbolisms that can be appropriate for all of us – the white horse is a symbol for the soul, and the brown horse represents the personality; water symbolizes one's emotions and is usually presented in dreams about being at the seaside; scenes that are seen on the left are things we are not conscious of, and those that we see on the right-hand side we are conscious of; the way we drive motor cars in our dreams are the way we are driving our lives, or aspects of our lives; we are all travellers in Life, so hotels and the people in them can be the people with whom we are associated, etc. People in our dreams are usually aspects of ourselves – mother and father can symbolize the personality and the spirit aspects of ourselves, the friends in our dreams can represent certain characteristics that we have, etc.

Meditation is a wonderful way of receiving guidance. You need to be able to be still, withdraw your attention from the world without to the world within, calm your emotions and hold your mind steady. This is not easy. Having done this you then need to listen with your inner hearing and see with your inner eye for any visions. These are usually presented in symbolic form and you need to work out what they mean.

Fear and desires distort what you see in meditation.

It is only after the third initiation that one has direct and constant inner guidance from God, and a telepathic connection with one's guide – a master in the inner government of the planet.

Because we are in school, and therefore have to work things out for ourselves and exercise our free choice, the guidance we receive from God and our guides is usually given in the form of hints, instead of explicit answers.

YOUR PERSONALITY

—

Your personality is made up of the physical-etheric body, the emotional body and the mental body. It can therefore be seen as threefold, or it can be seen as fourfold (physical, etheric, emotional and mental bodies) with the abstract symbolism of a square.

The Whole of Creation is Light vibrating at different frequencies. It Is God's Song and is constantly dancing in cycles and rhythms. All of Creation is essential Life in manifestation.

God's Creation is divine, or sacred, on all levels. Your personality is a perfectly created God made instrument for the purpose of incarnating. You did not origin-ate from the mater-ial world. You came from the Heaven world, beyond time and form, and incarnated into the mater-ial world of form and time.

God manifested this Creation and it is not an illusion. That we have mistakenly identified with the Creation, and not with our Source, is an illusion.

You need to become aware of, develop and master this wonderful equipment, so that your instinctive nature, emotions and mind do not run away with you or overwhelm you. You are like a charioteer who needs to learn to guide your three (or four horses), instead of having them gallop off with you.

You need to learn the difference between what you instinctively sense, what you feel, think and know.

Your personality needs to be developed and made into something strong and enduring. Through our talents and through experience we refine our bodies and expand our conscious awareness. With practice and greater awareness we can improve our performance.

As we bring ourselves up in conscious awareness, step by step, refining our bodies in the process, our personality needs to adapt to the higher vibrations. Ultimately the personality is there for you to carry out God's Purpose and Plan on Earth, in a loving and wise manner.

The form aspect mirrors where we are at in conscious awareness. What we are not getting together within is reflected without in the form world. What disturbs the personality are our unresolved problems.

The Mother aspect provides the personality and nourishes it. This means that **the Mother needs to be respected**.

"Spiritual" puritans regard the matter or Mother aspect as beneath their touch, dirty and evil. This attitude prevents them from coming to terms with aspects of their personalities and mastering them. Matter, the feminine, is the polar opposite of spirit, the Father aspect. She is not anti spirit. She is not bad or evil. To say that God's Creation in matter – God created forms – is sinful, dirty and evil is to say that God is somehow sinful, dirty and evil, which is absolute nonsense. Puritans have un**natur**al, unclean ideas about aspects of Life. What is anti spirit and bad is humanity's ego (see Chapter Six). Making out that matter is evil is an attempt to dump one's ego onto Mother.

Nobody can master your bodies for you. **You** have to master your own personality. If you think that you are going to master and uplift your physical, emotional and mental vehicles into the light by ignoring them, putting them down, oppressing, whipping or violating them or with any other punishing, loveless approach you are mistaken. It is unwholesome to oppress or deny any part of your personality. You cannot rise above Mater, in conscious awareness, until you love and respect Her.

We need to wake up, gradually, to the fact that we do not have to be ruled by any aspect of the personality – physical instincts, emotions or mind – and that ultimately it is an instrument for service for the One Life.

The most valuable earthly asset that you have is your personality. Treasure it. It is the only one you have. Without it you cannot incarnate. If it is harmed beyond repair you have to leave the physical realm.

The personality needs to be respected and correctly taken care of, otherwise it gets damaged. If you do anything excessively you will most

likely injure your personality in some way. Learn moderation in what you do. If you go to any extremes you will most likely, at some stage, have to swing to the other extreme to get the balance.

If the personality is continually polluted and abused it dies. If the Mother, the Earth, is continually polluted and bombed by humanity She will die too, so what is the point of this mindlessly stupid and criminal activity? Does Creation, including the mineral, vegetable and animal kingdoms, deserve this treatment? What useful or creative purpose does this serve, especially as our earthly lives depend on Mother Nature? Humanity needs to learn to work **with** Mother Nature.

THE PHYSICAL-ETHERIC BODY

The physical body is sustained and contained by the etheric body. The etheric body is a mesh of lines of light.

There is nothing peculiar, sinful or superfluous about the physical body. Every aspect has a purpose.

The human physical body has certain instincts that are similar to animal instincts. The first instinct is to survive. The instinct to survive is the will to be reflected in matter. For this it is necessary to find a territory in order to obtain a food supply. Having established this it is then safe to procreate the species and to rear offspring. To reproduce the species is the second instinct. Defending one's territory and one's children is natural. There is nothing unnatural about our instincts. If it is necessary to kill a life-threatening intruder, or invader, the instinctive nature in us will do so.

The physical body instinctively knows. Where there is love and wisdom, which are harmless, the instinctive nature has nothing to fear. If someone is killing you in a subtle way, for instance psychological abuse, you may, at some point, want to kill the culprit. This is a natural self defence response. However, what needs to be killed is not the person but the person's destructive illusions that are being used to destroy you.

Sex is a perfectly natural God-made act. Sex is the beautiful union of a male and a female that allows for the continuation of the species and the production of a physical body for an incarnating soul. Sex is a beautiful experience, if the two people engaged in it love one another. It is an opportunity for them to express their love for each other. The moment sex is used as a form of pleasure, entertainment, as a cheap thrill or is in any way perverted it becomes an utterly meaningless and empty experience. Rape is a power game and an act of unnecessary violence.

Puritans have the grossly distorted idea that sex is a sin or evil. It is their idea about sex that is evil, not sex itself. It is man's disrespect and misuse of sex that is sinful and disgusting.

If all of humanity practised celibacy the human race would be discontinued.

Sex means getting together, union or at-one-ing. You cannot get your world together, your life together, in conscious awareness, if you think sex is dirty or revolting.

The physical body maintains itself providing it has sufficient water, food, fresh air, exercise, sleep and sunshine. It is able to heal itself, but if discordant notes, in the form of illusions, are ceaselessly sounded out the personality will be continually distressed and dis-eased and will then not have the chance to heal.

Listen to your body. It will tell you, non-verbally, what it needs and what food it requires.

Indulgences weaken the personality. The physical body can be trained by you to have bad habits, for example drug or alcohol addiction. Any substance that is foreign to the body is a toxin, and the body is open to becoming addicted to toxic substances. It does not get addicted to health-giving foods. If you have trained your body to be addicted to some toxic substance you will, when you decide to give up the bad habit, have to re-train your body to do without the substance and the habit.

Our eyesight (day vision), teeth (no fangs to tear meat with), saliva (alkaline), jaw movements (side to side) and the length of our intestines all indicate to us that we have vegetarian digestive systems.

Through our sense perceptions – sight, hearing, touch, taste and smell we register what is happening in our environment.

Pain indicates that we are doing something wrong and that there is an important lesson to be learned. The moment we have corrected the mistake the pain goes away.

The physical body works in rhythms and cycles. This is why it responds to the sound of drums and music with distinct rhythmical beats. You need to get in tune with its tempo and not force it to work differently. Be inconsiderate to your body and it becomes tired, irritable and sorry for itself. You stress it if you push it to hurry. Hurry it and it goes out of step with its own natural rhythm and makes mistakes. If you treat it badly it becomes distressed and if you exhaust it, it suffers from depression.

Discipline applied without love and wisdom is destructive.

If you listen carefully to your instinct you will find that it does not lie to you. When it senses, for example, that something is wrong or that a person is not to be trusted, find out what it is telling you.

The instinctive nature does not fear God, Life, the real. It is Created by God, Life, and Life is loving. It is afraid of the ego and other illusions. (This subject is enlarged on in Chapter Six.)

The instinctive nature fears when it knows that you are not handling something correctly, or if you are not taking responsibility for what is happening. It also fears when you indulge in negative thinking and imaginings, which are quite unnecessary. Tell your physical body terrifying things and you will terrify it. Fear is another indication that something is amiss. It prevents us from getting on with things. We do need to find out what our fears are and do something to overcome them. Let the fears of your physical body indicate to you what you need to work at.

Birth is the beginning of a life cycle in manifestation, which culminates in "death". What is birthed is your new physical vehicle and it dies when it completes a life cycle. You cannot die. You came from eternal Life, the Heaven world, beyond time and form. You "pass away" from your physical-etheric vehicles at the end of a life.

When we pass on we take nothing except the experiences we had and the knowledge we gathered from the experiences. We cannot take our "belongings" with us, as they ultimately belong to the One Life.

The function of the physical body ultimately is to carry out God's Plan and Purpose on Earth.

Man's evolution begins on the densest level of Creation – the physical-etheric – and the inner journey continues up through the next two levels – the emotional and mental planes.

When we are no longer ruled by our physical bodies and our conscious awareness is ready to extend beyond the physical-etheric plane we take the first initiation. Thereafter our conscious awareness is focused on the emotional body.

Initiations are degrees of expanded conscious awareness of Life that we achieve. They are the curriculum for humanity in this School of Life.

THE EMOTIONAL BODY

The emotional body is on the next level up from the physical-etheric body. It is more subtle and vibrates at a higher frequency to the physical and etheric bodies.

Your emotional body registers feelings and any desires that you may have. You need to learn if you **really need** what you desire.

The emotional body is discoloured by the discordant desires of the ego, the separated "self".

Your innermost feelings sense the truth. If you listen to them you will not be led astray.

Mastering our emotions is nothing short of a Herculean task. We need to master the emotional body with the use of the mental body. Our emotional reactions and upsets are bound up with our ideas, or beliefs, of what is right or wrong in all areas of our lives – social behaviour, religious conduct, etc. We react to the things we **think**, or judge, are wrong. Other people, however, may very well be doing something they **need** to do, in which case it is not wrong. What they have done is upset our belief systems, which may not contain much truth.

Ideas are conceived of on the mental level. In order to expand your mind you need to be a free thinker and to question everything, including your social and religious beliefs.

When we have done something wrong we **know** deep within us. The mistakes we make in Life and the mistakes that other people are making with their lives can also upset us. All mistaken behaviour can be rectified if the original idea, behind the act, can be traced, examined and discarded and replaced with a harmless idea. The problem, having been solved, no longer upsets and disturbs us. The emotional body is then calmed and the instinctive nature is no longer alarmed.

If our emotions run away with us we get lost in our emotional reactions. This is what we need to take charge of and master.

Suppressing our emotions is no way of mastering them. If you are repressing or avoiding them you have no chance of examining them or of maturing emotionally. Emotions that are held in and unexpressed are one of the main causes of disease. They need to be expressed harmlessly.

When we have sufficiently matured emotionally the emotional body is the vehicle through which we express love.

When we have mastered the emotional body, which is symbolised by water, we take the second initiation. It is at this stage that the heart chakra opens, and we have learned to love. We "fall in love" with Life and become Life's lover. This initiation is a sublime experience and is far more potent than the first. It is at this initiation that the personality and soul come together, at-one, and we dis-cover our true identity for the first time.

At each initiation, Light from above comes down through all our bodies. With this light we can see our mess, on the plane that we have just mastered, more clearly. This then has to be cleaned up. As we expand our awareness the intensity of the incoming light, that we receive at initiations, increases. Each initiation is more powerful than the last one. The light that we are filled with, at these initiations, facilitates a quantum leap in consciousness. Thereafter our progress is more rapid.

The cultural idea that white Anglo-Saxon men are not allowed to have any emotions is cruel. They are brought up to believe that they are not allowed to cry, i.e. express themselves emotionally. As a result they have little chance of maturing emotionally, taking the second initiation and expressing their love openly.

While in the process of taming our wild emotions, we develop and expand our minds. Having done that we reach up onto soul level and register our true identity with the One Life. Our conscious awareness, having grown beyond our emotions, is then focused on our mental body, so the next step is to tame, or master, our (lower) mind and at the same time awaken and unfold our intuition (or higher mind).

Each time we graduate from one level of Life and move on to the next we experience a sense of withdrawal, a kind of death, followed by a birth into a new level of consciousness on another level.

THE MENTAL BODY

The mental body, symbolized by air, is on the mental plane and is more subtle than the emotional body. It vibrates at a higher frequency to the emotional plane.

Your mind is the vehicle which allows you to carry out your actions and purpose. From the plane of mind we rule our individual world or lives. The magician's tool is the mind. With our minds we can create ideas or thoughtforms, which define our course of action and our conduct.

The mind is the tool that we use to understand the principles of Life and the truth consciously, which we can then apply to our practical lives and build into our worlds.

The intuition, or higher mind, and the mater-ial mind, (which works with thought material – ideas, or thoughtforms), working together give us the opportunity to link the Heaven world and the mater-ial world.

In order to develop your mind and your powers of thought it is necessary to learn to think for yourself. You will most likely, at this stage, have intellectual pursuits. As long as you have some authority out there telling you what to do and what to think you will not use your mind. If you do not use your mind you cannot make decisions, so you are not free to run your life and others will run it for you.

The only way you can be free is to have a free mind, be a free thinker and exercise your free choice. In order for you to be able to work out how Life does and does not work you need to be able to think for yourself.

Free-thinking people, i.e. the ones without any external authorities, question everything. This is necessary if you wish to find out the truth. You have to ascertain the truth for yourself. Humanity has accumulated mountains of mistaken ideas about Life, reality, so it is essential to question everything that is presented to you. Is what I am being told true or nonsense? The moment you believe an idea to be true you give it power. The nonsense that we learn has to be unlearned at some stage. What is the point of conforming to such ideas?

You need a free, open, empty mind to find out the truth. In order to have a free, uncluttered, open mind you need to get rid of any fixed points of view, fixed ideas, rigid idealism, judgements, definitions, illusions and limiting behavioural patterns. For example, "All men are gross, male chauvinist pigs." "I only talk to other Christians. We know-it-all." "I will never . . . " "This can't be the way it is. It should be [ideally] that way, because I want it that way." We get trapped by limited thought-forms. **You** created them or adopted them from other authorities. The thoughtforms did not create us!

Fixed ideas and ideologies and beliefs – religious, political, etc – are what people go to war over, unnecessarily.

Obviously as we climb up the mountain of matter, in conscious awareness, our points of view change. From small mindedness we expand into broad mindedness and have a much wider view of Life, until eventually when we reach the summit of the mountain we can see all points of view, i.e. the whole picture. Having then a 360 degree view of things it becomes impossible to take sides, because the view encompasses all, so you are on everyone's "side".

The moment we identify with an idea we get trapped in it (see Chapter Six). A concept of something is not the actual thing. For example, my idea about a daisy is not the daisy. Life itself is not a human concept.

There is no rigid blue-print for living Life. You cannot live Life within the confines of a thoughtform, or try to control Life Itself with the intellect. You cannot contrive Life. Life was here before you had any ideas about It. When we contrive things with our minds we cannot flow and allow things to unfold naturally, spontaneously. We are here to learn to understand Life and act in harmony with that.

Ideals are concepts. Instead of living in concepts live in reality, Life. Conceptualizing your life interferes with the living of it. A realist is someone who is willing to work in tune with Life, what is.

If you identify with your mind you get stuck in it. If you get stuck in your mind you are not free and you cannot attune to Life. You are beyond your mind. You are the one that is using your mind.

You can choose which thoughtforms you wish to work with. You can "change your mind" – the ideas in your mind – whenever you choose to. The mind is like a computer – you can put any ideas (programs) you like into it and take them out whenever you decide to. The ideas we have "brainwashed" our minds with colour our vision and determine the way in which we see things. For example, you are a white person and have the unreasonable idea that whites are superior to all other non-white races, so when you look at non-whites you see them as beneath you. A huge section of God's Creation, of which you are a part, is now beneath you – so you think – which is ludicrous.

Your frame of mind determines your point of view of Life. What you **think** about Life, whether it is true or mistaken, affects the way you perceive things and therefore your experience of Life. We reap what thoughtforms we sow. A dreary attitude to Life will give you a dreary life experience. If you wish to see clearly you need to get rid of your illusions and be prepared to face up to the Truth and find out more about Life.

In order to know if an idea is true or false you need your intuition, or higher mind, which knows directly. The idea will ring true or false. You can also bounce ideas off your innermost feelings to find out if they feel right. Your awakened heart can tell you if an idea is loveless and harmful or not. Learn to hold your mind steady in the light of the truths that you have found.

Thoughts are like seeds. If they are nurtured they grow. We give them power if we create them as meaningful and important, as then we pour our Life-force energies into them.

Our negative attitudes to life, for example, "I give up," "I can't," "Life is impossible. It sucks. Poor me," etc, are of no earthly use to anyone and are unrealistic. They hold us back in bondage, demoralize and depress us and lead to failure. The practise of negative thinking is not in any way useful. Our negative mindsets work against us. With positive thinking one can make the mistake of covering over a negative thought with a positive one, which means that the negative idea is still there. Negative ideas have to be removed and replaced with truths. This means that one has to be a **realistic** thinker.

Much of the time negative thinking is an excuse to avoid reality.

Our limited, impoverished, ugly, illusionary ideas about Life and ourselves distort our minds, distress, depress, dis-ease, destroy and kill our personalities, other people and the planet. They also blind us to the real, to what is really happening and prevent us from thinking clearly.

Illusions are denials of reality and are hideous dis-harmonies. They cast dark, toxic clouds over our lives. They are the spells in the fairy stories that have to be dispelled. Reality is perfectly beautiful. Replace all your Life-negating thoughtforms, which are nonsense, with realities, truths, and your world will be filled with light and joy.

You need to bring your conscious awareness and your mind up into the light, the truth, the real, to eradicate illusion. You do not have to have any ugly ideas about Life Itself, anything, anyone and yourself. They are toxic, not true, not necessary or useful and they weigh and bog you down. They are heavy burdens to carry.

Any Life-negating thoughtforms that you may have bring about your own downfall. They are the hell experience. Hell is not a place. Hell is a frame of mind, here and now. Life is not a state of mind; It is not what you **think** It is.

We do not succeed in Life with Life-negating thoughtforms.

"Insane" people are not really mad. They have fed their minds with insane making, maddening ideas. When the mad ideas are released balance and sanity are restored.

The mind is potent. We can be extremely harmful with our minds. There is no need to have any fearful, Life-negating ideas. What causes chaos is man expressing his ignorance. We wield and direct energy through our thoughtforms. We express ourselves via our thoughts and energy directed through a Life-negating idea is highly destructive. Essentially everything – the Creation – is in perfect order. You cannot change what is. You can change your ideas and attitudes and, in doing so, heal your personality and change your whole life experience. Our life experience is coloured by our ideas and attitudes (refer to "Solving Problems" in Chapter Five).

You are in charge of your mind. You can have whatever thoughts you choose to. You do not have to be trapped in any ideas. We can get so tied up in our thoughtforms that we lose sight of reality. You can create what you choose to with your mind. Sow a beautiful thought and you will experience beauty. Sow a horrible thought and you will reap horror.

Nobody can change your mindsets for you. You have to find out what mindsets you have. You have to do the work to drop them and replace them with truths.

You can find out what ideas make up your world and change all of them, if you choose to. Ask yourself what you think about any aspect of Life. You can find out where and when you got certain ideas. All the events in our lives are recorded in our memories. If we ask ourselves, "Where did I get that idea from?" what happens is a memory comes to mind of the experience, when we formed the idea.

The mind does not know the truth. The intuition registers the truth. Without all the facts, in a given situation, we arrive at wrong conclusions with our reasoning mind. This is why the intuition, or our innermost feelings ("gut feel"), and heart are needed to guide our reasoning. You can ask yourself what you **think** about a situation, and then ask yourself what you really **feel** (and this does not mean desire) about it. The answers can be completely different.

To access your ideas about a situation you can ask yourself how you see it. You may find out that your attitude to it is negative, and therefore depressing, but you can change your whole approach to one that is optimistic and useful, one that you can succeed with. It is all up to you. You can be creative with negative experiences – for example, a loved one is "dying" of cancer – and turn them into a positive learning experience, just by changing your attitude.

The answers to our problems are not found in the mater-ial mind. They are found on the plane of the intuition and can be arrived at through the process of meditation. The Facts of Life are not in the intellect. The intellect can understand the Facts of Life.

You have the creative power to build thoughtforms. You also have the power to dispel them. They do not have to own you. You are responsible for your thoughtforms.

If we base our lives on untrue, unrealistic thoughtforms – illusions – then we suffer. If we base our lives on the truth, the real, with love for Life, we experience joy and happiness.

You have trained your personality to accommodate illusions. They have become built-in habits. Your personality is conditioned by them. When you get rid of these illusions you have to re-condition your personality. This requires a great deal of inner work.

Rooting out the weeds in your mind is like going through the layers in an archaeological dig. As soon as you have uncovered one artifact, and

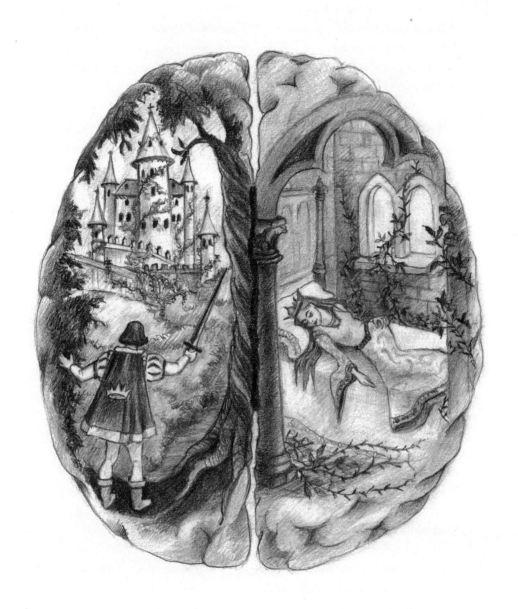

dispelled it, you are able to see more clearly. You are then able to see the next thing that needs to be brought to the surface and lifted up into the light. Illusions are dispelled in the light of the truth. You need to become aware of all the thoughtforms in your archaeological dig so that you can sweep your mind clean.

If you do not "change your mind" Life presents to you the same lesson over and over again, until one day you wake up, experience a dis-illusionment and learn the lesson. Then your ideas and perspective are changed.

When you have cleaned up the illusions that you put into your mind, that you deluded yourself with, and the illusionary roles you thought you had to play out, the possibilities are then limitless. You are no longer trapped in limited ideas.

Your mind, together with your intuition and your heart, assists you to discern the real from the unreal consciously. When you are able to do this you can free yourself from illusion and live in the Real World consciously. We do need to know our true identity and what we are not.

We also need to learn to act wisely. This we cannot do until we have worked out, with the use of our minds, guided by the intuition and the heart, how Life does and does not work.

The lower mind, referred to as the left brain, and the higher mind, or right brain, have different capabilities, which can be enumerated briefly as follows:–

Lower mind	Higher mind – the intuition
for the material world – form	for the spiritual world – formless
receives impressions from the form world	receives impressions from the Heaven world
for thinking with	with which we know
deals with time, relativity	operates in the eternal now
deals with the mater-ial world and registers forms isolated and separated from each other	registers truth and the Heaven world registers the whole
with which we can understand logically . . .	. . . what the higher mind registers

cannot register your true identity as that is beyond Mater – cannot extend beyond form, material aspects, the personality	with which we know our true identity
can describe form, things, external realities	registers spiritual, internal realities
cannot describe Essential Life	
differentiates, analyses details, dissects, divides, separates	sees the whole, wholes, patterns and how they relate
interprets our feelings and our instincts	
assists us to realise consciously what is taking place, a tool to gain conscious discernment . . .	. . . with the guidance of
does not know – needs to be informed, interprets truth	directly knows the truth, reality
a tool to create thought-forms with	

With razor-sharp discernment you can cut through the cords and chains of bondage, which are the imprisoning thoughtforms.

Scientists have explored the mater-ial world with the use of their lower minds. To find out about the more subtle levels of Life it is necessary to use the higher mind and the inner senses – inner seeing, inner hearing, inner smelling, inner touch.

When one has mastered one's mental body, which is another Herculean labour more arduous than taming one's emotions, one takes the third initiation at the top of the mountain of matter. This is when the inner journey Home is completed and one births the soul – the Son, the Christ child or Buddha nature, symbolized by the sun – in conscious awareness.

One cannot climb the mountain of matter and free oneself unless one has balanced one's masculine and feminine energies, and until one is using one's lower and higher mind. The balance and equilibrium of the two provides a sound base for light to pour in and for one to reach soul level.

Because one has just worked through the mental plane and illusions, it is after the third initiation that one can consciously dispel the ego entirely. It is not possible to enter the kingdom of Heaven if one is trapped and earthbound in illusion.

At this initiation the ajna centre opens, which allows higher telepathic communication. After this initiation the son has direct guidance from God within via the spirit aspect at all times, as matter has been transcended and the alignment of spirit, soul and personality is then unobstructed by the ego.

Once again one shifts onto another level. One's conscious awareness, having extended beyond the mental plane, then focuses on soul level, and one begins another cycle of expansion in consciousness.

The third initiation is the beginning of the training for planetary service and the higher initiations.

RELATIONSHIPS WITH PEOPLE

P eople are all aspects of the One Glorious Life and God's Creation and are therefore essentially beautiful and wonderful. They need to be loved and respected and given a space to exercise their free choice, discover their talents, to get on with their individual lives, to fulfil the purpose they came to Earth for, to grow up, work out their own salvation and evolve.

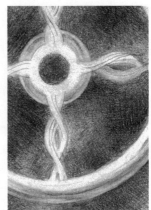

Humans have been given an innately good nature. It is the mistaken ideas that humans conclude about themselves and Life that distort their thinking, behaviour and their lives.

What happens to others is their free choice. Everyone is entitled to do exactly what they choose to do. What they create for themselves or do not do for themselves is up to them. Their free choice has nothing to do with you, unless it directly affects you. People have to fight and win their own battles, bring themselves up into the Light and find their own way Home, without the interference of others.

Depending on their motives people can be of great benefit to others and the world, or a destructive force.

You cannot change anyone. You cannot make or force anyone to do anything. People learn through Life experience. They are convinced by experience, if they are willing to learn from it. People have to change their own minds.

What makes a relationship work is love and truth. Without love and truth no relationship can survive. You cannot truly relate without love. You cannot have a healthy relationship with those who do not love themselves and who deceive.

What does not work in relationships are illusions and the deceptions and nasty, destructive games of the ego.

Basically there are two kinds of people – the givers and the egocentric grabbers. The givers are true to themselves and are Life's lovers. They are truthful, reliable and contribute to others. Grabbers are Life's egocentric whores that prostitute everything for their own selfish gain. The grabbers are users, usually dishonest and in no way benefit society. The lovers are constructive, creative, supportive, consider the whole and do worthwhile things. The grabbers demoralize and degrade others, destroy and kill, are avaricious and do hideous things. Grabbers couldn't care less about Life and the Creation. They are not committed to Life, so they are not responsible.

Life's lovers stand for the truth and the light. They love you for what you are. Grabbers are deceptive, have blinded themselves and blind others to the truth and the light. Grabbers only "love" you for what they can get out of you.

Lovers do not play harmful games. They can be trusted. Egocentrics are hole-y terrors that are against Life, cause chaos and wars and wreck everything. They cannot be trusted. Egocentrics have cost humanity countless billions with their lawlessness and wars. They are in the process of destroying the entire planet with their greed. They are blind to the fact that if they kill all the nature kingdoms off, and the planet then becomes extinct, they will have absolutely nothing left. There will be no food, because they will have turned the Earth into a desert. They may have a pile of money somewhere, but there will be nothing to purchase. They will not even be able to purchase another planet.

The crying shame is that humans do not have to be egocentric grabbers. They can drop their egos (see Chapter Six). People are not their egos and their egos are their own worst enemies.

Unwary givers that have no discernment get trapped and used by sly grabbers. Grabbers believe that they are separated from the One Life and do not realise that they are aspects of the One Life, therefore if they prostitute others for their own gain they have prostituted themselves. What we do to others we have done to ourselves.

The givers find the Way. The grabbers get themselves lost in the dark.

Givers have healthy relationships – there is giving and receiving on both sides. Egocentrics have unhealthy relationships, in which they do all the taking and devouring and give absolutely nothing but abuse. Healthy relationships are effortless; unhealthy ones are heavy, painful and exhausting.

The relationships of lovers survive because they are cared for. Egocentrics play such nasty games that they break their relationships with others. Who wants to play painful games and suffer indefinitely? Grabbers break people's trust in them. Once trust is broken the relationship cannot continue.

Egocentrics forfeit all their relationships. They are loveless and possessive. Possession is stifling and imprisoning. Egocentrics lose all their "loved ones".

We are not here to dance attendance on and please other people's egos or try to impress anyone. We are here to be true to our real selves and get on with our mission in Life.

The people who love are the people who hold the fabric of humanity together.

While addressing a person, love and support his or her real self. Ignore the egos and acts of others. Then you do not support their nonsense. If you take people at face value you get taken in by their acts. You do need to see a person's act and the actor behind the act.

Those who believe they **are** their images and acts are out of touch with what is really going on inside of them. They are split between their fantasy and reality.

You need to accept where people are in terms of growth and conscious awareness, and what games they have chosen to play. There is no point in resisting where they are and what they are doing, because that **is** where they have arrived at. They are not going to fit into the roles you and others want them to play. Why should they if they do not want to?

If you have decided that what someone else is doing is not in order for you, you will have no peace. With acceptance comes peace. You can, however, point out to people that what they are doing is of no benefit to them and tell them why, without trying to make any choices for them, control their actions and dictate to them. You do not have the right to dictate to anyone. You can sprinkle seed ideas around a person's free space without intruding. If they choose to accept or reject what you say that is their choice.

The moment you step over the halfway mark in a relationship, in an attempt to force, control or dictate, with good or bad intentions, you have invaded a person's space and the person's right to a free choice. The person will either become aggressive with you, so a war between you is begun, or avoid you. When an animal is cornered it will either fight to the death, if necessary, or run for its life. It is fighting to survive. In the same way, an invaded person will put up a fight for her or his right to exercise her or his free choice.

If you allow people their free space, free choice and their illusions and approach them in a non-aggressive, caring way they have no need to defend their space and point of view. Then there is no war between you. Do not trespass on other people's lives, space, property, karma, etc. You are not responsible for anyone else's free choice. You cannot protect people from Karmic Law. You are responsible for your free choice and your actions.

Do not attempt to interfere with anyone's life. Let people come to you, if they choose to.

Are you making a safe space for people to be with you, or are you being possessive, judgemental, critical, aggressive, abusive, controlling or dictatorial? If you are do not be surprised if others avoid you. On the other hand, is the person you are with giving you a safe enough space for you to share and express yourself in? Be'ware (be aware) of the games other people are playing.

If you respect others and truly care about them there will be the end of war.

We are aware of the pain others inflict on us. We are mostly unaware of the pain we cause others, as we are not on the receiving end. Do you want to increase the pain on the Earth?

Disapproval, antagonism, a spirit of revenge, hatred, criticism and gossip do not work. They do not resolve anything. Revenge is childish. Good will, loving and compassionate action dissolves enmity and heals relationships.

If someone has invaded or trodden on your free space you do need to put the person in his or her place. When you do this you make sure your space is respected. If you are too soft people will walk all over you.

If someone irritates us we have to take responsibility for our own irritation. If we put the blame outside of ourselves we will continue to be irritated, i.e. the problem will not be solved.

The best thing that you can do for anybody and any living creature is to be a loving friend. When you respect others and acknowledge them you are demonstrating that they matter and they count. They do not have to take up arms and declare war on you.

When you respect others you are, in an indirect way, telling them that they can respect themselves. People who have no self-respect treat themselves, others and Life detrimentally.

People do not need to be criticized, shouted down, judged and condemned or rejected. They do not need to be made to feel stupid for their mistakes. See **why** people do things. They need to be understood, guided and educated. Humanity doesn't yet know and needs to become enlightened. People are ignorant and therefore make thousands of mistakes, without realising, initially, that they are doing anything wrong. People do what they are doing because they do not yet know any better. They may have a vague sense that something is not quite right.

You cannot tell anybody anything. They have to find things out for themselves through experience. People only change their behaviour with a change in consciousness.

To say that a person **is** "a rogue", "feeble", "revolting", etc is not true. The person is playing out the game, role, of a rogue, a feeble or revolting character. You can see the nonsensical games that people are playing out, experimenting with, without judging them.

Life's lessons – experiences – make us grow up, if we are willing to learn them. People attract to themselves the lessons they need, so do not stand in their way.

People are making mistakes, "sinning", all the time. They are not their mistakes. They are not a mistake God coughed up. "You **are** a miserable sinner," is a judgement that says you **are** a mistake. You may have mistaken ideas about something. These mistaken ideas are not you.

Many people think they know what they are doing, but they are not really conscious of what is going on. Do not assume that people are speaking the truth and know what they are really talking about. Those who pose as knowers, and are not, are a danger to others and themselves.

Dictators and controllers impose their will on others and do not allow them a free choice, free will. They try to take charge of the lives of others, demanding obedience, and, in doing so, take away their freedom and suffocate them. Any person that does not allow others a free space and the chance to be true to God within is some kind of thief. On the other hand freedom requires responsibility. Irresponsible, lawless people have to be controlled.

Romantics and idealists live in a fantasy world. Idealists expect you to fit into their dream. If you do not you are discarded.

Materialistic people are only concerned with matter. They are usually elitists. There are three kind of elitists — material snobs, intellectual snobs and religious snobs. Materialists disregard the spiritual aspect of Life and the Heaven world, whereas puritanical, "spiritually" orientated people disregard and snub matter, God's Creation.

Fanatics are not open to other points of view. They think their "truth" is the one and only truth, which they defend. People who identify with their points of view and their beliefs have territorial attitudes to them and are ready to fight to the death, if necessary, to keep them.

People are not fully responsible until they have grown up. Immature people look for people to parent them, tell them what to do and take charge of their lives. Immature men want a mother figure to take care of them. Immature women find a father figure to protect and look after them.

Irresponsible people are a burden on society. They refuse to take responsibility for their lives and their choices and get nowhere. They refuse to face up to and look at their failures and their folly. They do not correct their mistakes. They expect others to take care of them, tell them what to do, make their choices for them, carry them and their karma, redeem their mess, fight their battles and get on with their lives for them.

They pretend to be helpless, pathetic powerless babies, which then means that you are obliged to parent them. This is a trap. They intend to make full use of you and rob you of your freedom. This is unfair to you and does not give you the chance to get on with your life. It is not selfish not to be available for these people, with whom you can only have an unbalanced relationship – you do most of the giving and most of the work. **They** are the ones that are being selfish.

Do not allow other people's problems to become your problems to solve. That is their work. You can suggest things to them, if you choose to. All people are required to account for their actions and to be accountable for them. It is the law.

The kindest thing that you can do for people who refuse to grow Up is to tell them to get on with their lives, and not consent to play a parental role for them. If you play a parental role you encourage them to continue to be irresponsible and a heavy burden on you. If they don't have a parent figure fussing around them and trying to please them, they are put into the position of having to get on with their lives and grow Up.

If others refuse to play their part do not be tempted to play their part and fill in for them. Irresponsible and fearful people expect others to go over the halfway mark and be overly responsible, take care of them and do for them what they are too scared to do. They exhaust their care givers. Going over the halfway mark makes you over-extend yourself, which can throw you off balance and put you into the position of self-neglect.

Do not allow anybody to set you up to play out what they desire you to play out for them. If others cannot accept you as you are and what you have chosen to do, that is their problem. If you care what other people think of you, you can make the terrible mistake of being true to what they desire of you instead of being true to your real self.

A lot of people who refuse to get on with their lives are afraid to. Many fears, when examined, turn out to be groundless, if not ridiculous.

It is actually impossible to help those who refuse to take responsibility for themselves and their lives. They **will not**, i.e. they have chosen not to, get on with their lives. They will therefore remain in the quagmire they got themselves into. If you are not careful you may get bogged down in their mess with them. Step right away and withdraw your support, because you are wasting your precious time and energy. They will find all kinds of excuses for not getting on with their lives.

It is impossible to work with people who are not truthful about their failings and mistakes and refuse to face them. Assisting those who are willing to help themselves and take responsibility for themselves is a joy.

People who are negating themselves, for example, "I am no good," "I hate myself," "I reject myself," not only drag and hold themselves down, but they also drag others down with them. People who do not love themselves do not help or uplift themselves. They destroy themselves and those around them. Self destructing people, with sick ideas about themselves, cause havoc and put others through hell. They have unworkable relationships and lives. It is impossible to uplift anyone who is putting himself or herself down. Pitying someone who is self-negating opens you to their hell. Pitying someone doesn't help the person at all.

We are not separate from each other. What we are doing to ourselves we are doing to others and the whole planet. What we are doing to others and the planet we are doing to ourselves, because we are all aspects of the One, inseparable Life.

People who have dreadful relationships with themselves do not rely and depend on themselves. They depend and lean on others, as they are not self-supporting.

Those who have been demoralized and destroyed by others underestimate themselves, are brought to believe that they do not deserve anything of Life because they are so inferior, or "bad", and that they have to prostitute and martyr themselves for others.

You need to look at what kind of people you are attracting to yourself. If you are playing out, for example, a self-sacrificing martyr you will attract the opposite type of person. In this case it would be a selfish egocentric. It is not necessary for you to be stuck in this role forever.

We seek, consciously or unconsciously, to balance out our relationships with others. If one person is too frivolous, the other person will polarize into being too serious. If one parent is too strict with the children, the other parent might be too lenient, to compensate.

Relating is like ballroom dancing. It is necessary for the two of you to do complementary steps and not tread all over each other. You do not have to dance with clumsy dancers. You have a free choice.

Do not allow anyone to take you over and own you.

It is useless to compare yourself with another person. We are all unique and have different things to work out.

If you love Life, respect yourself, sincerely care for others and have genuine good will towards them their negative and destructive thoughts about you will not reach you.

Essentially Everything is in perfect order. Our relationships are also whole. People, however play unhealthy games with each other, mistreat others and deceive. The way to keep a relationship clean is to tell the truth and clear, or confess, and apologize for the things that you have done wrong, and refrain from playing deceptive, mean games with others.

LOVE

Lovers of Life are committed to Life, the truth, reality, the real because they love It. They are realists. Loving Life they love everything to do with Life and the Creation. They are true and faithful to Life.

The Ten Commandments, which tell us what not to do, are all expressions of respect; respecting and loving Life.

Love is naturally harmless, compassionate, healing, nurturing, respectful, patient and considerate. It lets go of people, allows them to be free, free to be true to God within and does not interfere. It is supportive, preserving, encouraging, constant, enduring and does not require to be pleased. It is not sentimental. Love gives joyfully and unconditionally without any thought of reward. It benefits, enhances and increases the lives of others.

Unconditional love gives others the space and the freedom to be. It does not criticize or judge and punish. Neither does it play manipulating guilt games and make people feel bad.

It does not demand obedience through tyranny and fear. It liberates.

Because love is harmless and sustaining where love is fear is not. Where there is love desire is not.

Love is not elitist and does not put others down with criticism, gossip and judgement. It does not fault-find even if it does see the mistakes people are making. Love is forgiving and inclusive. It is not soft-hearted or hard-hearted.

Love does not attach itself to anything. It is not a leech. It is detached.

Love is indestructible, timeless, eternal.

Parenting

Children need to be loved and respected. They need to be free. They belong to the One Life and are essentially whole units of Life. They are not our possessions.

They need to be nurtured, protected, housed, clothed, educated and guided. They need to be prepared for Life. The best a parent can be is a loving friend and educator, not an interfering dictator. Self-destructing parents destroy their children with them. The worst parents are psychological rubbish dumping, destructive, terrorizing dictators.

Are you creating a safe space for your children to flourish in? If not do not be surprised if your children lie to you and reject you.

Children that are not disciplined and are allowed to run riot do not feel secure. To feel secure there has to be some kind of order.

Most educational institutions prepare a child for a form of employment. Schools and universities do not teach children how to solve their problems or impart any wisdom. They are not wholistic and do not prepare children for Life. Children are required to take their lower minds, their memories and their muscles to most schools. They may leave their emotions, their hearts, their souls and their spirits at home, because these are not catered for. Most schools are spiritual deserts.

Because children are not taught to come to terms with their emotions and handle them, many of them try to drown their sorrows in alcohol and drugs later on in Life.

What happens in many schools is that your performance and your high marks are more important than you are. If your marks are low or average you leave school with no sense of self-worth. There is practically no compassion in these highly competitive establishments.

Having spent most of their lives at a desk the children have had very little opportunity to learn to relate and to communicate, yet the society depends on the stability of the family unit.

The child does not receive an wholistic education at the majority of schools. Unfortunately some parents expect the schools to teach their children everything. They teach their children little.

Children are not brought up to honour and cherish the planet and the nature kingdoms – the Mother aspect. They are not brought up to have spiritual values and honour the Father aspect. Many are brought up to be competitive materialists who can rape the planet.

Highly ambitious parents also push their children to be high achievers, and if they do not succeed they are made to feel no good, worthless failures. This means that the child is not taught any self-respect or self-worth by their parents and their schools. They can break their children with their ludicrous expectations.

Egocentric parents expect their children to make a human sacrifice of themselves, dedicate their lives to their parents, achieve impossible feats in order to enhance and please the parents' egos. "My son/daughter got a first class matric with twenty distinctions and a hundred gold medals. [Aren't I the most wonderful parent in the whole world?]." These parents rob their children of their lives.

Neglected children are taught that they do not count and that they are unimportant. Parents who are over-attentive teach their children to have exaggerated self-importance. Interfering parents prevent their children from finding their feet. Impossible parents make the lives of their children impossible. Problem parents do not allow their children to get on with anything.

Irresponsible, loveless parents, for example alcoholics, do not parent and guide their children. Abusive parents are careless. They punish, damage and destroy their children. They cripple their lives on a subtle and/or physical level. They teach their children that they have to be disrespected and punished in Life for no reason at all. These children do not know how to value themselves. They are too damaged and destroyed to succeed.

Irresponsible, immature parents are often parented by one of their own children. The parent that requires parenting from a child prevents the child from having a life of its own.

Parents who expect their children to please them and make up for their disappointments in life, do not allow their children to be true to themselves and get on with their own lives and purposes. They deprive their children of their freedom. Children cannot make up for the disappointments parents have created for themselves. The children are not the cause of their parents' problems.

When parents pass judgement on their children and resist what they are doing, they hold them captive in the very thing they do not want them to do. The judgement they make is the thoughtform, or spell, they hold their children in. For example, "My daughter **should not** do this! I do not want this to happen to my daughter and me." These thoughtforms are traps as there is no acceptance of the situation and neither is there a solution, or alternative.

Possessive parents do not want to let go of their children and allow them a free life. Dictatorial parents do not acknowledge that their children are free children of Life, with unique destinies to fulfil.

A MATURE
RELATIONSHIP

A mature relationship can only take place between two people who love one another, and who are responsible. Immature people play irresponsible and silly games with each other, because they do not yet know love. Egocentrics play disastrous games.

In a mature relationship both people are free, have equal rights, are true to themselves and God within. They give each other a space to work and grow in, i.e. they do not possess and therefore imprison each other. People confuse possession with love. People are not our belongings.

Both give willingly, and receive and share. This is balanced. If one party gives too much the relationship goes out of balance.

Both are realistic, i.e. they do not base their lives on illusions. Their lives are based on the truth, the Light, so their relationship endures.

Relationships based on lies – illusions – end up being a farce; they do not work and cannot endure.

Each take 100 per cent responsibility for their own lives and their own actions. This means that neither has to play a parenting role. Because they are mature they can stand alone, knowing that they are complete in themselves. Neither imposes their will on the other. Each plays his or her part in keeping the relationship healthy and in good order. They work on a group consensus basis, based on what is best for all concerned. It is balanced and fair. Thus both thrive.

Neither puts the other one down. There is equality of the sexes. Whether we have feminine or masculine physical vehicles we are aspects of the One Life, in incarnation, so how can one be superior and the other inferior? The sexes, or dualities, are of **equal** importance. If this were not the case then Creation would be out of **equi**librium.

A mature relationship can only work with two self-reliant people. Then they can both stand free as individuals, without either one being some kind of burden to the other. They do not demand anything from each other and they do not intrude on one another. They give each other the space to explore, to breathe and to fulfil their purpose.

There are no pretences or acts. They are both simply themselves.

Because the relationship is open and honest they can discuss the problems that arise and work out the solutions together, on a group consensus basis. They work as a team. Their relationship is not static and dead. It is alive and growing. Egocentrics are not capable of being honest and open, and they are not safe because they use, abuse and destroy others. Without truthfulness and honesty there is no real relating and communication. There is no growth, no discoveries of what is. A relationship in which both use deception becomes a polluted, unhealthy relationship.

As both are loving and giving they are supportive. They back each other up effortlessly and are able to realize their inherent potentials.

Only responsible, whole givers can enjoy such a relationship. Selfish people are out for themselves only, without any consideration for anyone else.

The synergy in such a loving relationship is powerful, strong and light.

Your Other Half

People make the mistake of identifying with their physical vehicles. This means that they then identify with the sex of their physical vehicle. "I am a man," or, "I am a woman," people say, not realizing that they have actually announced that they are half of a person. Having done this they then look for their other missing half, out there in another person.

What we essentially are is a ball of Life-Light, a spirit. Essentially we are whole, complete, units of Life. You were born into this lifetime as a whole person. There is no such thing as half of you being in another person, when you are both essentially whole.

Let us say that you have found some wonderful person who you believe is **your** other half. "I'll die if she or he leaves me. She or he is my life." It is blatantly obvious that this is nonsense, because if she or he does die you do not automatically die with her or him. Your whole life continues. Nobody is the beginning and end of your life.

If you create someone else as your greatest love, more important than Life Itself, what you have done is made a god of the person. This idol you place before God and your spirit self that you have divorced yourself from. You have disempowered yourself, having decided that you are helpless without this idol. If you should lose this great, romantic love, the end of the world you created will come about and you will be devastated. What you have created is a melodramatic, tragi-comedy!

The idea that someone else is **your** other half means that you regard the person in question as **yours**. Possession is not love. "He is mine," "She is mine," are imprisoning illusionary statements. Love sets people free; it does not hold anything or anyone captive. Nothing is ours. When we pass on we have to leave everything behind, because all things belong to the One Life. In reality you cannot possess anything or anybody.

If you see another person as your other half that you cannot do without, you are using that person as some kind of filler or addictive drug. That person is supposed to fill in the big holes of your illusionary incompleteness, and make you happy. This means that you totally depend on that person to make your life work, so you are unable to stand free.

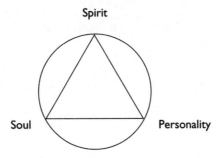

We are complete units of Life. The circle can symbolize completeness and a unit. Within this unit are a number of attributes – the spirit, the soul, the personality (mind, emotions, etheric-physical body). A triangle – the Trinity – in a circle or the Celtic cross can be used to symbolize this.

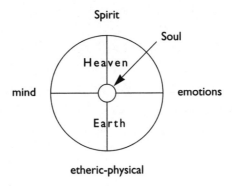

The love that we have lost and are looking for is **our** other half that we separated and cut ourselves off from. **Our** other half is not out there; it is up here, on the vertical arm of the cross.

If we believe that we are the physical body only, and that somehow the mind and the emotions also come into this, then logically what we have done is separated ourselves off from our souls and our spirits and the Heaven World. (This is dealt with more fully in Chapter Six). We have cut ourselves in half and concluded that we are only a half of a complete unit of Life. We have now lost our other half. So then, this is all that we think we are:—

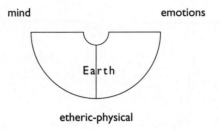

mind   emotions

Earth

etheric-physical

Obviously we will feel a deep discontentment and dissatisfaction. We will then try to find our missing half. Thinking that we will find our true selves, our other half, in an ideal mate of the opposite sex or a soul mate out there, in someone else, is a big illusion. The soul does not have a sex and does not mate with other souls, neither did your soul come in a half. Your physical body wasn't born in a half either. We cannot substitute our other half with another person. This is a ludicrous attempt to make ourselves whole, when we are already essentially whole.

You do not have to go looking for your great love out there, or search the planet for your lost self. Your eternal love is your other half up there, relative to where your conscious awareness is, here and now. People get the horizontal dualities of the Celtic cross muddled up with the vertical dualities. Your great love, that you are missing, is all of Life Itself.

You cannot be someone else's other half. Someone else cannot be your other half. You do not need to depend on someone else to complete you and your life, and therefore make your life work for you. Other people are your travelling companions.

Your love "affair" with Life and God is the most important relationship you have. If you love Life you love all.

What we need to marry, or at-one with, is our own other half. In conscious awareness we need to raise matter, our personalities, to Heaven. When spirit and matter come together in our conscious awareness the marriage of Heaven and Earth takes place within us. The two worlds become one. The symbol of this is the six pointed star with a circle around it. The two triangles represent the Heaven and Earth worlds.

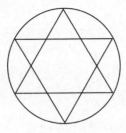

The marriage of the prince (the spirit) and the princess (the person-ality) in the fairy stories takes place **in ourselves**. In some of the stories the prince represents the lower, active, mater-ial mind and the princess symbolizes the higher, receptive mind.

RELATIONSHIP WITH LIFE

Life Itself is perfectly glorious, whole, complete and free. Essentially Life is a "sea" of blissful being and is sacred. Life is a celebration of being.

This Creation is enchanting and delightful. All aspects of Life are inter-related and inter-connected – inseparable – as this is One Life. We all belong to the One Life. There is really nothing else but Life.

There is nothing wrong with Life. It is divine on all levels. The way reality is Created, ordered, Is just the way it all is, whether you like it or not. Accept what is and get on with that, instead of trying to impose your limited ideas onto reality.

You have been given the greatest gift of all – Life. The richness of Life comes from simply being and enjoying all of Life. If you did not exist you would have nothing. When you have life you can experience everything – abundant Life.

You are a child of Life. Whether you are a human, or an animal, or a plant or a rock you are a child of Life.

Commit yourself to Life. The more you put yourself into Life and the more you truly give the more you receive from Life, so why not give of yourself 100 per cent?

The feeling of Life Itself is exquisite. Treasure every second of Life. You will not repeat any moment of your life. You cannot recover the time that you have spent. Spend time usefully then you do not waste your life.

You cannot avoid Life, as you are an aspect of It. You need to play Life by ear, because it is a happening. You cannot capture Life and make It dance to your desires and concepts. Life is not an intellectual game or a human concept. It is a glorious happening to be enjoyed and experienced.

You need to find out what Life is about and work in harmony with that. We are not here to try to catch Life. We are here to live it.

The only life that you can get on with is your own. You cannot get on with someone else's life.

If you do not have love and respect for Life you will not enjoy it, neither will you be able to free yourself. Your quality of Life depends on your attitude to Life. If you are feeling miserable it is because you have some useless attitudes towards Life. The irresponsible blame Life. "Life is mean to me," they say, when it is their mean attitudes that have landed them in the situation they find themselves in.

We need to learn to love Life unconditionally. "On condition that I have a spouse/a child/an expensive car/a house/a yacht/etc. I'll be happy." Having created it this way this is what you will experience – unhappiness, until Life gives you what you desire. When we are empty of preconceived ideas and conditional desires of the ego we are flexible and free to be here now, in the moment, and to take action from our essential selves, i.e. we are not trapped and conditioned by our thought-forms.

When you really love Life you are on Life's "side". Then you are **for** everyone and respect everyone without trying. You feel good will for all of Creation and wish all living beings to succeed. Life's lovers are friends to all.

If you judge Life you will have no peace, and you will not make your-self happy. There is no such thing as an ideal state of affairs, as things are in a constant state of growth and movement. You cannot fix Life into an ideal.

When we go against Life, on an ego mind trip, we experience dis-satisfaction in Life. We can only feel complete and content when we acknowledge that we are part of the Whole and accept that we are aspects of the One Life. Life is not dull and boring. The human ego is dull and boring.

Your ego separates you from Life, so you lose the sense of belonging. It fights against Life, which requires a great deal of effort and is very painful. This slowly wears your personality out, eventually killing it. In order to step in tune and in harmony with Life, here and now, you have to go through an ego death.

Without an ego we can surrender to Life, what is. What is the point of combatting what is?

The illusions that we believe in separate us from Life, because they are not the real. You cannot experience Life fully when you are trapped in them. Illusions make our lives impossible, as they are impossible. Life is not hell. Our misunderstandings of Life are hell. To be able to get on with Life properly we need to be free of illusions.

If you build your life on illusion you are bound to get hurt and dis-illusioned. If you build your life on reality, the truth, you build your life on a rock. Then you do not fall and hurt yourself. You can succeed.

We suffer in Life because we do not know how It works, who we really are, what our equipment is made up of and how to apply ourselves appropriately.

The way you treat Life is the way you treat yourself. If you mess with Life you will get yourself in a mess.

Negative attitudes to Life and yourself will make your life a hard struggle. Focusing on the negatives – illusions – makes you feel sick and depressed, and apathetic towards Life. If you give up on Life you give up on yourself. If you give up on yourself you give up on Life. You are not separated from Life. Life is eternally here, so there is no escape from it, even in suicide.

Some people, having abandoned their unhappy lives, try to live through others. We all have to live our own lives.

What we want to happen and think ought to happen, and what is **actually** happening, much of the time, are worlds apart. Even if you cannot see it everything in your life is there for a purpose.

The moment you have a concept, for example, about how swimming should be it gets in the way of swimming and finding out more about it. When you swim, swim. You can't swim in your head.

Let things be just the way they are, i.e. do not resist what is going on. Accept exactly what is taking place. What is happening now is what **is** happening now. Resisting that is exhausting. Desiring anything else and refusing to accept what is unfolding does not help you in the very least. Many of our obstacles are our attitudes, non-acceptance and the refusal to come to terms with what is happening. Out of acceptance comes peace and the opportunity to deal with what is taking place in a creative way.

Expectations limit one. They are usually ideas about how we desire things to be for us. Expect things to be just the way you find them, then you will not be disappointed.

We cannot change the world that God Created. We cannot improve Life or control It. We can control our minds and our behaviour, change our attitudes to this Creation and improve our abilities with practice. With the right attitudes we can enjoy Life to the full.

Let things unfold before you and you will find that decisions will present themselves effortlessly. You will know what to do if you are in touch with what is going on. You are not in control of Life. You are contained within the order – Laws – of Life. Therein is your security. You need to learn about Life consciously and get on with That.

The more we try to control Life the more we interfere with It, and the less things work for us. Life works perfectly, so why not give up trying to get Life to fit into your contrivances and plans?

If you listen to Life now and are in harmony and in step with It then your life is effortless. Everything comes and goes at the right moment in time. When you are present, now, paying attention, with a silent mind, you make no mistakes, as there are no distracting voices going on inside. When you are ready for something it comes naturally without force, so there is no stress or strain. Trying to force something to happen requires enormous effort. In order to step with Life and work in harmony with It you have to be a realist. There isn't really anything else to work with.

The most important step is the one you take now. You cannot take a step at any other time. Now is the only time that anything can happen. You **can** only live now.

The only way you can successfully achieve anything in life is to have a vision and intend to complete it. Without intent we do not surmount our difficulties and find the way through. An intention sets up a vibration, or note, which attracts the experiences you need to fulfil the vision. An insincere intention does not work because it does not carry the right note. You cannot fool Life. We need to direct our lives with harmless, sincere intent.

In the real world there are no illusions and nonsensical beliefs. Your illusions and nonsensical beliefs are wrecking your quality of Life.

It is not necessary to have a belief system about what is. For example, the Earth is a sphere or globe. This is a fact, not a fiction. Either you **know** that the Earth is a sphere or you don't know.

If you try to impose your theory on how to live Life onto Life, your theory will distract you from what is actually taking place.

There is a time and place for all things in Life. There is a time to expand and reach out, a time to digest and inbreathe; a time to dance and a time to sleep; a time to laugh and a time to cry; a time to rejoice and a time to be quiet.

If you walk and only see your feet you may walk into a tree. If you walk and only look into the sky, you may stumble on a rock. Step with the light shining over you, your awareness encompassing the sky above, the path before you and the Way ahead.

Ultimately we need to learn to relate to the Whole of Life and co-create with It. In reality we are related to all – the One Life – and are in perfect relation to all. You do not have to go anywhere to embrace Life. What you have to do is give up imprisoning illusions about It.

When you are **for** Life you can experience bliss, joy, happiness, love and contentment. If you go against Life you experience suffering, misery, pain and discontentment.

Life cannot die. Life is not dead, so there is no need to be afraid of "death" or passing on (to the next level of Life).

Your love "affair" with Life is the most important relationship you have. It embraces all. Your family is the whole of Creation, all of Life.

LIFE'S LESSONS

We are all students of Life whether we are aware of this or not. There is only one teacher – Life. Life is the perfect school or workshop. Allow yourself to be a disciple of Life. Life is the best teacher. Life's teaching is through experience and does not always come in words.

We came to Earth to explore and to work out what is in conscious awareness, to learn to love, to become wise and then to co-create God's

Plan on Earth. In order to become consciously aware of reality, Life, i.e. a knower, you have to pioneer the frontiers of your being and go on a voyage of discovery to replace your ignorance with knowing.

The most perfect training you can have is Life training, while listening to God within and being true to that. God within you is your ultimate and very best authority. God Knows all. Humanity is ignorant. You have to be willing to learn from Life experiences, lessons. This school of Life works for us if we allow it to. We are all unique individuals and we are all receiving our own individual Life training.

We all have to learn our own lessons and do our own homework, i.e. earn our own knowledge and wisdom. Nobody can realize or understand our lessons for us. People can tell us things, but we have to see and realize them for ourselves. What you need to learn now is right in front of you.

Understanding something intellectually from a book does not mean that you know. What that means is that you have understood someone else's knowledge. It isn't **your** knowledge. You can read one hundred books on how to ride a horse and understand what is said, but you cannot pretend to know anything about riding until you have ridden a horse. Life education is a living experience. Some people dress up in other people's knowledge, appear to be knowledgeable and mislead the unwary.

We need to eradicate our ignorance by finding out about Life and become loving, wise knowers; masters. We get to know through experience.

Life will demonstrate something to us, through life experience, over and over again, if necessary, until we understand the lesson. Unresolved problems and unlearned lessons cannot be buried or dumped and forgotten. You still have to learn them. When we understand something completely all doubt is erased. Knowing beyond a doubt allows us to stand firm. Then we are ready for the next step or lesson.

Karma is the sum total of unlearned lessons. We make thousands of mistakes because we do not know any better. This does not mean that we are bad, miserable sinners. It means that we are ignorant. We cannot **be** bad if we are sparks of Life. Because we are creators with a free choice we can get into the habit of bad **doing**, or of doing good. If people were intrinsically bad they would not be able to see the light and reform.

Life's education, which is experiential, is a process of perfecting your conscious awareness of what is. You cannot start off with perfect conscious awareness and not make mistakes or sin.

In order to register what is happening, during an experience, you need to be present now, paying attention, with an open, quiet mind, empty of preconceived ideas, so that you can see clearly what is taking place. When you are present now you can respond appropriately.

You have the ability to reflect and can reflect on an experience afterwards. You cannot correct the past or re-live it; it's past. If we mentally digest our experiences, or lessons, we can learn from past mistakes.

You cannot solve your problems if you refuse to acknowledge and admit that you have any problems in the first place. This is why it is essential to be truthful with yourself. Not finding solutions to problems is depressing because then there is no hope. Finding the Way and the Light is an exciting adventure.

If we resist Life's challenges they will most likely knock us down. Be creative and make a breakthrough instead of experiencing a breakdown.

Our hardest experiences are the most challenging and give us the greatest opportunity to learn and grow. They do not have to overwhelm us. They push us to go deep within to find the solutions, which expand our consciousness.

We cannot overcome a problem unless we first know what it is. Our lessons, problems, may overwhelm us at times. They seem to be insuperable, but they are not. There is the right solution to all problems and we are bigger than our problems. When we do not find the solutions we can get extremely frustrated and angry. Anger is the outcome of frustration. We have to and can find the answers. They are there.

If you steer unwaveringly towards the truth you will always find the right way through every situation, lesson. The truth liberates.

We can ask God for help at any time. Help will come if we need it. If not it can mean that we have something to work out on our own. We have to do our own Homework. We are Guided in the right direction and given hints, but we have to do the work. God is not going to learn our lessons for us.

Sometimes we succeed in learning and sometimes we fail. If we do not face up to our failures, learn the lesson and rectify what we are doing then we just repeat the mistake over and over again, get stuck in a rut and go round and round in a circle.

At times the same lesson is partially repeated as we didn't get that little bit quite right. Lessons have to be completely learned. We have to see the whole picture and we have to get to the heart of the problem, at the centre; the bull's eye. When you get to the crux of the matter, the point, you break through into the light, the truth, on the level of the intuition and find the solutions.

The sure indication that we are not doing something right is pain and misery. When we do get it right the tension, pain and misery disappear.

When you don't understand the lesson, your answer to the problem or the conclusion that you arrive at, doesn't add up. Your answer is nonsense. When it is right it rings true within and it makes logical sense.

When we solve a problem we learn something about how Life does and does not work and expand our conscious awareness. As we expand in conscious awareness we discover more and more about Life, reality, so our experience of Life keeps broadening and becomes richer and richer. There are always so many entrancing and interesting things to find out about Life.

What you need to do with the raw material of an experience is to extract out of it Life's Teaching and the lesson or lessons. After each experience ask yourself what the moral of the "story" is, the principle, what did and did not work during that experience. In this way, if you are prepared to learn, you will see the valuable lessons and gain true knowledge about Life. This is alchemy – out of the crucible of life experience you can transmute your ignorance into the gold of conscious awareness and wisdom. Only when you have learned a lesson completely and digested it thoroughly can you internalize it and utilize it. What you then need to learn is how to apply this new knowledge practically. You will receive a rich Education in this way and eventually learn wisdom.

By the law of attraction we attract the lessons we need. The more we are tested and tried the more we find out about ourselves and Life, and the more we mature. Our tests are challenges. They bring with them discontent, and send us on a quest to solve the problems. To solve the problems we have to find out more about Life and expand our conscious awareness. When we have an insight and release an old perspective our vibrations change. We can then attract a new experience.

We are constantly realising new things about Life, so we need to be constantly watchful and aware. We need to give ourselves the time to adjust to these new realities. Evolution is not instant.

The dark areas of our ignorance need to be replaced by conscious awareness of what is. Every lesson learned brings more light into your world, until all of your dark ignorant world is filled with the light of the truth, and you become fully enlightened on the level that you have been working on and take an initiation. You can then move onto the next level.

Growing Up and evolving is natural. You do not have to force it or interfere with it.

Life's lessons expand our conscious awareness and make us grow up. The more knowledge we gain, the more responsible we have to be. We can only become wise when we can discern the true from the false, the real from the unreal (illusion). When you know what is and what is not you can stand steady in the Light and not be led astray.

SOLVING PROBLEMS

We live in a world of dualities. It is necessary to see things in dualities, paradoxes, because Creation is based on the male (positive) and female (negative) complements; the dual aspects of a balanced Creation.

We have to find the balanced way between the dualities, otherwise we may get caught on a pendulum swing from one extreme to another. Anything in excess results in an imbalance. Breathe out too much or breathe in too long and you'll kill your physical body.

Artists have to balance the "positive" form areas and the "negative" spaces in their art works. The negative areas are as important as the positive ones, and require just as much attention in the creation of the composition. The space inside a pot is just as important as the shape of the form of the pot. It is the synthesis of the negative and positive aspects that allows for a creation.

A useful method of ascertaining the midway point of balance is to work with a triangle. For example, you discover that you are wearing yourself (actually your personality) out with a built-in habit of trying too hard.

You want to find a more balanced attitude to Life. The opposite of trying too hard is apathy, so on the bottom left-hand side of the triangle you put "trying too hard" and add other associated words like "forcing", or "trying to please", etc. On the bottom right-hand side of the triangle you write "apathy" and other words that remind you of apathy, for example "I don't care", or "I give up". Then you need to work out the point of balance, the liberation point at the top of the triangle.

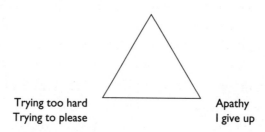

Trying too hard
Trying to please

Apathy
I give up

You may need to go into meditation at this stage to find out **why** you are trying too hard, in the first place. When you ask yourself, "Why am I doing this?" pictures of the past very often come to mind. For example, you see a picture of your mother, who is drunk. She tells you, "It's your fault that I drink. You make me unhappy." You believe her and conclude that you have to make your mother happy and please her. You try very hard to do this and end up trying too hard in all your relationships. You are trapped in an illusion and in a role. All this has to be unlearned.

The **truth** is that your mother has dumped her unhappiness onto you and has refused to be responsible for her life and her happiness. She has tried to avoid her misery with temporary oblivion, and has set you up to make her happy. The **truth** is that she is the one that is responsible for her own unhappiness, and that she is the one that has to solve her own problems, not you. The **truth** is that you are not the bad person, who has made her unhappy because you did not do anything mean or bad. Having seen this you can now give up trying to please her. The **truth** is that you do not have to please any irresponsible people who are displeased with their own lives, and what they have not done for themselves.

If you are not, any longer, going to play the role of the pleaser, that "did" something bad, how are you going to relate to others? Well, you do not have to swing to the other extreme and get apathetic. What you may decide to do is be true to your real self, and act from there, instead of running around pleasing other people and doing what they tell you to do, or what you think they want of you. At the top of the triangle you would then put "being true to myself".

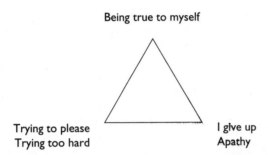

Being true to yourself then becomes your new practice.

Here is another example. You discover that you have an inferiority complex. Draw a triangle and write "inferior" on the bottom right hand corner. The opposite is superior, so you write "superior" on the bottom left hand side of the triangle. Now you ask yourself **why** you have an inferiority complex. The question, " **Why**?" gets you to the root of the problem. Memories of your father come to mind. Your father was a wonderful man who served the community in a positive way, which you admire. You admired all sorts of other things about your father. Being his son you made your father your role model.

You have spent your entire life comparing your achievements to your father's outstanding achievements, and have unconsciously concluded that everything that you have done is not good enough, so you have made yourself feel inferior. You come to realize that you cannot be your father. You can only be yourself. You can then look at your achievements without reference to your father. You discover that you haven't done so badly after all. You decide that from now on you will compare your current achievements to your past achievements to gauge if you are improving your abilities, and leave your father out of the picture. You are allowing yourself to be where you are at. At the apex of your triangle you could write something like "allowing myself to be where I am at".

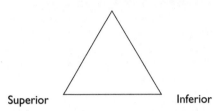

Allowing myself to be where I am at

Superior   Inferior

A mountain is roughly the shape of a triangle. When you arrive at the apex of the triangle you have found the light, surmounted your difficulty and liberated yourself from it.

Meditation is a sure method of solving your own problems and of lifting your conscious awareness into the light of the truth, providing you are employing your mind in the process. Sitting and meditating only, without any life experience to meditate on, will not expand your conscious awareness.

We can meditate on anything we choose to. Some examples are compassion, serenity, anger, love. Business men do informal meditations on specific problems that arise. We can meditate on any life situation that we may find ourselves in, or on the biggest question of all – "Who am I?"

The answers are all within you, on the plane of the intuition. When we meditate we can pierce through all the veils with our minds and focused intent, arrive at the crux of the matter and see the light.

Prayer is a way of talking to God and invoking Light. In meditation you make contact with God, be still within and listen to what God, or Life has to reveal to you.

YOUR TRUE IDENTITY AND YOUR EGO

Who are you **really**? We are made up as a Trinity – a spirit, a soul and a personality. These are the Father, Son/Daughter and Mother aspects of ourselves. The spirit, a spark of the One Life, existence, is **immortal** and is your true identity, the real self. The personality is **mortal** or ephemeral and is **not** your true identity. The personality is a **vehicle** that allows us to incarnate to have Earth experience. When the physical body dies we are still there, so we cannot possibly be our physical body.

The master Jesus identified with His spirit, the Father aspect, and told the people. He was accused of blasphemy, of being a false prophet and was crucified for coming to tell us the truth. He demonstrated that Life continues after death.

At this stage of humanity's evolution, in conscious awareness, most people are focused in the emotional body, an aspect of the personality. We can only register our true identity when we reach soul level. As a result, most of humanity **thinks** or assumes that its identity is the personality or form aspect and that the only and ultimate reality is the physical world, the Creation or matter. This belief is an illusion. There are two "worlds" – the formless world of pure Light – the kingdom of Heaven – where the spirit is, and the form world of matter – paradise, Earth, the Creation – where the personality lives. The soul mediates between these two "worlds" and links the two. These two worlds are not separated. They are only separated in the conscious awareness of humanity.

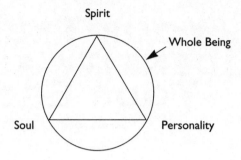

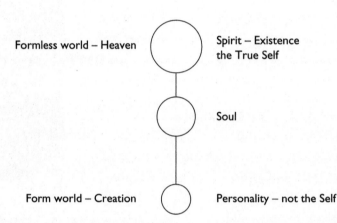

It is not surprising that we do identify with form while we journey through the form aspect, as our conscious awareness of Life, including ourselves, is not all that much expanded. At this stage we are developing our personalities and our attention is concentrated on this task. More than this society auto-suggests, with a confusing use of language, that we identify with the form aspect – "You **are** Angela," "You **are** five years old," "You **are** British," "You **are** a Catholic," "You **are** a doctor." All this is telling you that you **are** the form aspect. "I **am** going **to be** a doctor." How can you **be** in the future when you already **are** now?

If you do not yet consciously know yourself that does not matter. That you know that you do not know your real self is the truth. You cannot take a single step homewards without the truth.

If you believe that you are your physical body or your emotional body or your mental body and that this is all that you are, i.e. that there is no more to you, then you have separated, in your mind, your personality from your soul and your spirit. You have disconnected yourself, in your mind, from your Source, Origin, the Heaven world, so you are lost. You **think** that only the Creation is and that only the Creation exists, which means that the Heaven World does not exist in your mind. This also means you believe that you are dead when your physical body dies. This is another illusion.

The most subtle level of the form aspect is thought**forms**. If we identify with any concepts or thoughtforms we may have of ourselves, we have once again identified with the form aspect.

We appear, in form, to be individual only, unrelated and therefore separate. In essence we are all One Life. We are all certainly in individual physical bodies that are separated from other physical bodies. If we identify with our physical body then logically we are separate from the rest of all Creation. **The belief that we are separated from the rest of Life is another illusion and is the worst illusion that we can experience. It is the cause of all suffering, misery, distress, dis-ease and discontent.**

If I say "I **am** Angela Grey," it means that I have identified with my personality. When we identify with any aspect of our mortal personality and believe this is the ultimate and only reality of our beingness, i.e. ourselves, what we have done is **deny** and **negate,** consciously or unconsciously what we really are – the spirit, which is an aspect of the One Life, or existence. We are saying that we are **not** that. So what we have done, without realising it, is we have denied that we exist and that we are part of the One Life. This means that we must be dead, which is nonsense. This is when the people are turned to stone in the fairy stories and when the awful, nasty spell is cast, the spell which has to be dispelled eventually. This is when we go to hell, the underworld, which is not a place. It is a mistaken idea that we have created about ourselves.

The Creation is God's Song and if you believe that there is only the song then you have said there is no singer. When you identify with form only, or an act, what you are saying is, "I am the act, not the actor." This means you have cut the act off from the actor. You have said the actor doesn't exist. Only the act exists. This accounts for the term "split personality". The statement, "I **am** a doctor," means that I have identified with the **part** that I play in society – doctoring. Doctoring is what I **do,** not what I **am**. When I retire from my job as a doctor I do not suddenly die. I **am** still there.

This **idea** that we are separated from the rest of Life, that we do not really exist and that our true identity is not what it really is can be called the not-self, which in reality does not exist. In reality we cannot be separate from Life, our selves. When we believe that we are only the form aspect we have misunderstood reality or Life. Our understanding of ourselves is then downside up and front to back. We have to turn our understanding of reality – our true identity and where we origin-ated from – upside down, inside out and back to front.

Diagram of a person who Identifies with the Form aspect only

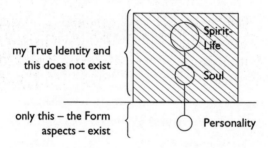

my True Identity and this does not exist

Spirit-Life

Soul

only this – the Form aspects – exist

Personality

When you cut yourself off or separate yourself from abundant Life you are lost in the forest of delusion where you cannot see the light. You are lost in the dark and imprisoned in the idea – thoughtform (the spell) – that you do not belong to Life. You disconnect from Life.

The idea of this separated, dead not-self which, in reality, does not exist is an illusion that humanity **made up** and created and can be called the ego. The ego is the monster in the myths, the cruel villain and the witch in the fairy stories. This monster that you **made up** is your **false** identity.

There is no such thing as death. There is only Life eternal. The only death there is, is the illusion of the separated "self", which does not exist. Losing your physical body does not mean that you have lost your soul and your spirit.

Your Ego – Your False "Identity"

Your ego – your false "Identity" – is NOT **the true you**. It is a mistaken idea about your true identity. **You** are not an **idea** that you have about your real self. It is an illegitimate identity or self. Because it is illegitimate it is a bastard "self." It cannot be anything else but what it is – a bastard. This bastard accounts for man's unnatural cruelty to man and the rest of this Creation.

The ego is nothing more than an entombing, distorted, nonsensical, human **idea or thoughtform**. In the final analysis it is nothing because it has nothing to do with reality. That is why the monster, the villain and the witch in the fairy stories, disappears at the end.

Do not blame Mother for your mistake of identifying with Her. "I have identified with my personality. It is the fault of my personality," is as ridiculous as saying, "I drove my car into the wall. It is the fault of my car." "I find that I am full of the desires of my ego, so I'll blame my emotional body and castrate it. I hope to dispel my ego this way." "In order to get rid of my ego I must ignore my mind. It is the fault of my mind that I have an ego."

When you try to impose an illusion – what is-not – onto reality – what is – what you are doing is trying to negate reality, what is. When you express your real self via your ego, or any other ugly illusions, your actions are destructive and evil. When you try to make out that you are your not-self or ego what you are doing is negating your real self, obscuring what is and pretending that your real self does **not** exist. In that case **your** ego is your own worst enemy. It is anti the real you. It is not only anti the soul or Son aspect, it is also anti the spirit, the Father aspect, and it is anti matter, the Mother aspect, including the Whole of Creation.

Our egos are killing our personalities and the rest of Creation – all of the nature kingdoms – with distress and dis-ease. It is the agent of dis-harmony, terror, de-stabilization, destruction, "death" of the form and death – non-existence – because it is non existent in reality. All it is capable of, because it is an illusion, is to destroy and kill the Mother aspect and obscure the truth, the spirit – your true identity – and the soul.

Good and evil is not really a duality. If you look at the dualities on the horizontal arm of the cross, for example male – female, red – green, warm – cold, summer – winter, and ask yourself which is good and which is evil you will see that good and evil do not apply. How can any aspect of God's Creation be "good" or "evil"? Is a diamond, or a carrot, or a tree or a horse "good" or "evil"? They are neither "good" or "evil". Are the dualities on the vertical arm of the cross – spirit and matter – "good" or "evil"? To say that the spirit is "good" and matter, God's Creation, is "evil" is ludicrous. Good and evil can only apply to what mankind **does**. Mankind's ego, which has absolutely nothing to do with reality whatsoever, which includes mankind, is evil and does evil things. Mankind is not essentially evil. The majority of people do not intentionally do malevolent and evil things. From the evolutionary point of view they are still immersed in matter and are the sleeping beauties, who do not know or realise what they are really doing in the broad scheme of Life.

The ego fights against Life Itself, God, Creation and your true self in order to try "to be". It sabotages what is and tries to invalidate reality in an attempt to replace it, but it cannot be because it is nonsense, the unreal. When you have an ego, a not-self, you have to fight it for the right to be your self. "Put Life and your real self off for me," says your ego. With an ego you are at war with your real self, Life, the truth, until you realize that the ego is an illusion which you can give up. When you give it – illusion – up, you find peace at last.

You are a creator. You created yourself as separate from the One Life and your true self. You are your true self and you have created a false bastard "self", so, on the one hand, you will create worthwhile things, but, on the other hand, you will, with your ego, practice black magic and sabotage your life, unless you intend to be harmless.

The penalty for having an ego based life and going anti-existence, anti-Life, by insisting that your ego is what is, when it is not, is that you have to live in hell. The ego is hell and as long as you insist on having an ego you are going to live in hell and be thoroughly miserable, lonely and in some kind of distressing pain. You cannot experience the beauty of Life, existence, if you are trapped in illusion.

On the way home to your real self, the truth, the One Life you meet your ego, which stands directly in your way. You put it there as a replacement of your true self. Your ego blocks out the Light and the Heaven world.

You are fooling yourself when you tell yourself that you are separated from Life. The ego plays the role of the fool. The ego cannot be anything but an act, a farce, because it is not the real self. Playing idiotic roles in absurd scenes isn't worth it – you cannot succeed. The idea that you are separated from Life and your real self is ridiculous, so, in the end, when you wake up to reality, you laugh loudly at yourself for "being" (playing out) such a fool.

When you give up playing the fool you can be your naturally playful, loving, joyful self.

CHARACTERISTICS OF THE EGO

The ego is only a mistaken human thoughtform that humanity believed to be the truth and that humanity breathed life-force, or energy, into and blew up like an inflated balloon. It does not have a brain, a heart, a spine, any nerves, eyes, or ears so it is mindless, stupid, heartless, spineless, insensitive, blind and deaf. It blinds you to the real, to your real self. In reality the ego does not make sense. The ego has no sense perceptions.

The ego is separated from abundant Life and therefore has nothing. It lives in an impoverished, Life-less (dead) void. It is impoverished because it is lacking everything – the One Life from which it is divorced. In order to make up for this poverty, having lost everything, and to experience some kind of satisfaction, the ego tries to **get** something **out** of Life, i.e. it steals from Life. It tries to fill the bottomless pit of the void, or abyss, it lives in with things – its possessions to which it is attached. These possessions are not only material objects. They include other people and intellectual knowledge. The ego even tries to steal the wisdom of others, dress up in it and pretend to be enlightened. The more possessions we have the more heavily burdened we become. But the ego can never be satisfied and content. It has no real content, so it is avaricious with an insatiable appetite.

Some people try to fill the void of their ego with alcohol and drugs and find satisfaction in the over-indulgence of food and sex. None of these things can fill this void and bring contentment. Only the reality of the true self can remove the void permanently.

The ego is nothing. It is of no importance whatsoever. It is therefore totally inadequate. So, therefore, it has "to be" a highly important someone. The ego pretends to be greatly superior, an impressive personage that requires the admiration of others who are supposed to grovel at its "feet", but actually it is a deadly dull, painful bore. There is nothing wonderful or interesting about it. This important somebody that you have made up is a make-believe "self".

Being Life-less the ego is powerless so it plays "God" – it knows all. The arrogant know-it-all ego actually doesn't know anything. It plays know-it-all because it wants complete control over others and to be their only authority. As it wants to rule it sometimes plays the king or the queen, and the rest of the cast is supposed to play obedient, servile subjects. Egocentrics can never admit that they are wrong or have made a mistake. They couldn't possibly have made a mistake because they know-it-all.

"I know the truth. Only I know what is best for you. If you do not follow and obey me you will never get Home," says the misleading ego. It places itself between you and God within you and takes you over, which means that it is preventing you from following your inner guidance and getting Home. If you have no authorities out there you can become Life's disciple, instead of being the disciple of some egocentric person, or group, acting an enlightened knower.

The ego cannot face the truth and will always deny it, because it is the not-truth. The ego is illusion, the unreal and the truth is the real. The truth dispels the ego, so it avoids the truth like the plague, whereas the ego is plaguing the whole of humanity and the rest of Creation.

In its separated, lonely world only the ego "exists", so it is all that matters. It has to be the one and only winner and all else loses. Nobody else matters, and God's beautiful Creation doesn't matter in the least. The whole of humanity and the whole of God's Creation can become extinct as far as the ego is concerned. The whole of Life, the real, has to sacrifice Itself for the ego, the unreal, so that the ego can "be". The ego can never actually be in the true sense because it will always be an illusion, what is not, although it poses as the real and distracts one from the real, as it is the unreal. It prevents one from getting on with the real, Life and our real selves.

It is nonsense, a pretended reality and therefore a deception. The ego cannot be anything but what it is – deception – so it is a trickster. It is nonsense, so it talks a lot of nonsense.

The monstrous, grotesque ego is the most disgusting, untrustworthy character part to play out, a pollution that is destroying humanity and the whole of Creation. You do not **have** to play out this role. If you do play out this role then you are not allowing your real self to play itself, i.e. you are not allowing yourself to be and express your true self.

The ego is fright-full and terrifies the personality that knows instinctively that the ego is a killer. When you have dispelled your ego and learned how to treat other people's egos you find that your fear is gone. The personality then knows that there is nothing to fear. It does not fear Life itself because Life Created it and because Life loves all. Love is harmless. The moment love is absent and there is danger (the ego) the personality senses it.

The ego is an evil character. Evil is the word "live" spelled backwards. The ego gives you a d'evil (of evil) of a time. There is nothing lively or lovely about it. It is a deadly, ugly devil. It is an "ugly customer" that pretends to be good and innocent. It pretends it is not doing anything wrong.

Being completely self-centred and heartless the ego is incapable of loving. It is vain and narcissistic. The ego is ruthless and relentless about getting what it desires to possess and will destroy and kill whatever stands in the way of achieving its ends.

THE EGO – YOURS AND OTHERS – IN RELATIONSHIP

Your ego is killing your personality, making you depressed and miserable, is causing you all your suffering, is imprisoning you in hell, is ruining your relationships with other people and Life, is killing your joy and is standing directly in your way of being your self and of getting home. Is it worth it? It is not possible to experience bliss, joy and happiness in hell. If you sacrifice your ego you will be free, joyful, happy, healthy, at peace and enjoying your real self and Life. The choice is up to you.

The ego is separate from all else, so you cannot really relate to someone else's ego because it is divorced from you. Besides it is so superior that you are beneath its touch. It pretends to be the "greatest" and you are a mere nothing. It is therefore quite impossible to have any kind of relationship with an egocentric.

Egocentrics are hell to live with. The ego sabotages relationships by divorcing itself from all others, i.e. by keeping people apart, separated. It cannot relate to Life as it is anti-Life, separated from It. It breaks you and others apart within. It cannot be wholistic or promote togetherness, as it is separative, so it breaks relationships apart and divorces people.

As it is stuck in its separated world it cannot see anything from anyone else's point of view. Your point of view is irrelevant. Only its point of view is "valid".

You are supposed to worship and please it and only it, i.e. you are not supposed to be true to God within, your real self. The expectations that egos have of others are cruel, inhumane and impossible. They break people.

The ego likes to be centre stage. It has to have the limelight and is more often than not dramatic, in order to attract attention. It wants all the attention and uses others as mere props for the drama it is acting out. The ego does not like anyone else to steal its limelight and be centre stage, so do not think that you will ever have the chance to shine with someone else's ego.

"I **am** Angela Grey [an illusionary concept of myself]. We Greys **are** superior to the Smiths, so we do not talk to them [says the family group ego]. We **are** Catholics and Catholics are the only religious group that knows the truth. All other religious groups are beneath us and do not know anything, so we are not prepared to talk to any other religious people [says the religious group ego]. We **are** British and the British are frightfully superior to all other nationalities, so we treat other nations like worthless pieces of dirt [says the national group ego]." (This example can be applied to any individual, family, religious group and national group that is ego-based.) Angela Grey has separated herself from nearly the entire human family. How is an Indian Hindu supposed to relate to Angela Grey? In reality Angela Grey is saying, "I, Angela Grey, an aspect of the

One Life, am superior to all other people, who are also aspects of the One Life." This does not make one iota of logical sense. Angela Grey, an aspect of the One Life, is as important as all other aspects of the One Life.

The aggressive ego is threatening, dominant, dictatorial and at its worst a tyrannical bully, a terrorist, that literally "gets away with murder" imposing its will on others. If you disobey it and refuse to submit yourself to it, it threatens you with doom and gloom warnings and death. In reality it cannot kill you because you are immortal, although it can kill your personality. It requires an obedient slave to carry out its orders and plans. In other words you are required to sacrifice your life, your free choice, freedom of thought, speech and movement. It manipulates with guilt, fear and terror. You are its prisoner.

The passive ego is the opposite of the aggressive ego. It plays a pathetic, moaning and groaning "Poor me," "I can't," "I am helpless," and, "If you do not do it for me you are mean and horrible and do not love me," game. It too manipulates with guilt. If you fall for this deception and agree – "Shame, poor you," – then you will land up being the slave of a passive ego. You are then its prisoner.

Both types of egos are possessive. "You are **mine** and I won't share you with anyone else. I own you, so you have to do what I want you to do." They want to take you and your life over. Possessiveness is not love. It is imprisoning. Love allows others to be free and lets them go. Egos **use** other people and whatever else to elevate themselves and to achieve their ambitions, so they prey on other people and their lives.

Men and women usually have an aggressive or passive styled ego, but the ego can change its tactics if it is not succeeding. For example, a woman can have an aggressive type of ego which may suddenly play the passive "Poor me," if it finds it necessary.

The ego is the war monger and is the cause of wars. "I desire to possess the country next door because I want its resources, so I'll just invade it with my army." "I want to take over the whole planet. The planet is mine, mine!", says a greatly blown up ego like the ego of Adolf Hitler. The ego can try to imprison and control Life Itself.

Egos come in different sizes depending on how much of their energy people put into their egos. Your ego is only as big as you created it. Some of them are small and others are spectacular depending on how much energy one has puffed into them. The bigger egos are the more dangerous they are. Irrespective of their size they declare war on others. These can be physical, emotional or mental wars. Small wars take place between two people who, for example, may refuse to speak to each other. All these wars, whether small or big, are unnecessary and extremely costly dramas.

If we confuse our egos with what we really are, and love our egos instead of our true selves then what we do is nourish and expand our egos.

In relationship the ego treats all of the Creation with total disrespect. It does not value anything. It gets a kick out of "cheap thrills" in any way it can. Sexually it is a cheap whore (male or female). Creation is there for its entertainment and, as it prostitutes and debases everything, it is a whore in all ways. It has no morals.

The ego wants a relationship to go the way it desires, only its way. According to the egos of others you are "good" if you obey them and a "bad", worthless reject if you do not. Nobody wants to be rejected. This is how it manipulates you — with emotional blackmail — to get you to do what it wants to get what it wants to get out of you. If you believe that you are "the baddy", when you have actually done nothing to deserve such a judgement, then you have become the victim of an ego. **It** is the baddy, not you.

The ego is incapable of apologizing for any of the nasty games it is playing and the deceptions it is using. Having no compassion it is unable to put itself into other people's positions and see things from their points of view. Nasty games and deceptions ruin relationships.

The ego is a blown up thoughtform of humanity, requiring energy to sustain it. In order to get the energy it vampires the energy of others and exhausts them. If you think that someone's ego is her or his real self then you give it power and support it.

The ego cannot relate to Life as it is non existent. Life is not impossible. It is the bastard ego that makes Life seem impossibly hard.

The male ego. Not all men regard females as inferior humans. However, a male who has a big ego sees a woman, at best, as second class, otherwise she is a mere nobody. In order to make out that he is vastly superior to her and a hero – "Mr. Wonderful" – he puts her right down, demoralises her and the importance of her sexual attributes, having forgotten that he spent nine months in his mother's womb, and if it was not for her he would not be in incarnation.

Putting her down, and her role in life, and destroying her in order to elevate himself hasn't anything to do with being wonderful, intelligent, heroic or more capable. There is nothing chivalrous, kind, loving and supportive about his attitude. Expecting her to be a self sacrificing martyr for his "glory" is disgusting. It is not possible for her to be happy or to succeed in a relationship with a man with such an attitude.

There is nothing superior about the male, or inferior. The idea that men are superior to women is an absurd and destructive illusion. There is nothing superior about being a woman or inferior. Women and men are of equal importance. "Mr. Wonderful" turns out to be an unmanly wimp, a bastard and a monster.

He plays her head, her authority, so that he can rule her. He usurps God within her and she is supposed to obey his dictates. As she is not free, is cut off from Life and her true self she is trapped in a prison. She has to give up her free choice and obey his separated will. In doing so he breaks her "spirit" or will.

Women are much better off being single than married to a sickening, dominating, killing male ego. Children too are safer without male egocentric bastards for fathers. The male ego is a menace to his family.

For centuries most men have been boosting their idiotic egos and going on power trips violating women and their rights, abusing, raping and killing them. This is not sane.

The male ego is strangling the whole of God's Creation as it regards the feminine principle as inferior, which includes Mother Earth. The male ego does not respect the Mother, the feminine aspect of Creation. She too has to prostitute Herself for his pleasure and his avarice, so he rapes, abuses and destroys Her.

THE PRISON WARDEN

Obviously it is necessary to remove criminals from society in some way in order to protect the rights of others. These people have committed crimes.

The ego's method of trapping and capturing innocent people and holding them prisoner in hell, illusion, is to **falsely accuse** them of some "crime" and judge them as guilty of **being** bad (worthless, inferior, no-good, a failure, etc, for some obscure, non-existent "reason"), so they get a false identity of badness. They must then make up for this terrible thing they have done, which in reality they have not done, by serving the ego. They have to serve a prison sentence and work for the ego. It doesn't matter how perfect your behaviour is the ego will always find fault with your method of serving it, which means you will never get off your prison sentence and the ego will have you enslaved and imprisoned for as long as it wants to use you. Of course, if you have not fallen for the false accusation in the first place you will avoid getting caught and avoid the prison sentence. The difficulty is this – if you do not know who you really **are** and someone accuses you of being bad how do you know if they really know if you are bad or not? If you do not know your true identity you may very well fall for the trap. If you know your true identity and are aware of the traps of the ego you will not fall for them, so you will remain free.

An ego can only trap you and hold you captive if you have allowed it to be your authority. If you do not know that another ignorant person does not know you may make the mistake of appointing this person, together with his/her ego, as your authority, in which case you have opened yourself to the dictates, machinations and victimization of this person's ego. You have given an ignorant person power over you.

The ego traps lives in order to make use of them. The trap and the prison is the thoughtform that you **are** bad in some way, which means that you are denying your true self. When you deny your true self you completely disempower – de-Life – yourself. The ego plays the trapper, the judge, the prison warden and traps you with an illusion, a false Identity – for example, you **are** bad. The trouble with playing the prison warden is that you have to stay in prison with the prisoner. If you **are** an aspect of Life Divine, which **is** What you really **are**, how can you possibly be bad? You may have **done** something bad – destructive – but you **are** not essentially bad. The verbs "be" and "do" are two different verbs. You can change what you are **doing**. You cannot change what you really **are**. You have to **be** first before you can **do** anything.

The ego pretends to know, to be enlightened, so that it can be your authority. Once you have allowed an ego authority – power – over you what you have done is opened yourself to and given yourself over to the dark forces, unintentionally. If you do not make an ego your authority it has no power over you.

The ego – yours, that of another or some group ego – plays the spirit, God within and the God that you have to honour and obey. It therefore cuts you in half, blocking out the light, the spirit within you, the truth and God and makes you turn against your true self. It implies in some way, spoken or unspoken, that God within you is a fraud and not to be trusted, because God is **not** what Is, that **it is** what is, the power and the glory, which is complete nonsense. Playing out "God", the power and the glory, it "therefore" has total control over you, and you do not deserve to have your life and experience Life and the glory, or to go Home to Heaven, which is also ridiculous.

"Believe in me, trust me," says the ego, "because if you trust your true self, God within, you will not obey me. I will not have control over you, I will not be able to make a slave out of you and use you to carry out my separated desires for me. You will be free, which means that you can exercise your free choice, which is, as far as I am concerned, a ghastly sin. So, do not be bad and be true to your real self, God within. Be good and follow me, only me. Whatever you do, do not serve the truth, the Light, God and God's Plan. God did not Create me. God is my worst enemy. God, the truth and the light destroy me. I have to distract you from the Light, God within, and blind you to the truth and God, so that I can possess you for my own ends. Worship me, not God, and grovel at my feet. I am the greatest, the power and glory. Let me possess you, destroy you and devour all your energies to sustain me. Let me vampire your whole life. Do not be mean and hold anything back. Sacrifice your real self, the truth, the light, God within, your life, Life, the real for me. I will never admit that I am a false 'light', a man-made, mistaken illusion, because then I will lose credibility and my power over you."

The dark forces slowly disempower and cripple one with self denials and self doubt, thereby obscuring God within, your real self. Having done this they can then take you over and use you.

The ego cannot love so it cannot forgive. "I will never forgive you for the 'crime' you committed." Often the ego accuses you of things you would not dream of doing. If you listen carefully you will discover that much of the time the ego accuses you of the very things it is guilty of doing. If you need to forgive someone you must have judged that person in the first place.

Another method of imprisoning others is to possess them.

VICTIM ROLES

The ego abuses and victimizes everything – the whole of Creation. We become the victim of our egos and the egos of other people, if we are not aware of them and the games they are playing. We can dispel our own egos and not be the victim of them, but the egos of others are still going to try to trap us.

Through our ignorance we fall into the traps of the ego. Once you have been caught by an ego you are required, by it, to play out certain game-roles. The aggressive ego expects you to play out the "martyr" and the passive ego expects you to play "Atlas" and the "rescuer".

The Martyr. You are supposed to fall at the "feet" of the aggressive ego, which is a dictator, worship it and make a human sacrifice of yourself for it and obey it. It threatens to kill you if you do not. It rules you with fear and terror.

Atlas. "Poor me, Atlas, I can't do it . Help me Atlas. I am helpless," says the deceptive passive ego. "Do it for me Atlas," it says. Playing helpless and pathetic means that one has no intention of uplifting and helping oneself. "Poor me," is a manipulation and is a heavy, depressing game that drags everyone concerned down. Nobody succeeds in this "sad" scene.

You cannot get on with another person's life for him or her, get on with another's spouse for him or her, sleep for others, eat for others, etc, etc, etc. You can only assist others to help themselves. People have to be responsible for themselves and their actions. You cannot take responsibility **for** them. If you fall for this trap, this lure with the response, "Poor you. I'll do it for you," then you have unwittingly collaborated with and become the slave of an ego. "You take responsibility for me Atlas, [not possible] then I can have a free ride on your back and you can carry me.

I am too little [deception] to be responsible for myself. If you leave me and get on with your own life, Atlas, something terrible might happen to me and it will be your fault for being so selfish and neglecting me [nonsense]."

You are supposed to worry about "Poor me." Atlas gets stuck and held back by a "Poor me" and cannot get on with his or her own life.

By holding oneself responsible for someone else (an impossibility) one does not allow oneself to be free. You do not have to rectify someone's wrong doings. You cannot do this for anybody. People have to rectify their own mistakes.

Rescuer. "Come and rescue me from my own choices, and my own folly [not possible]. I refuse to be responsible for my actions and my karma. Liberate me, while I do nothing, because you see I can't take responsibility for myself [deception]."

You cannot rescue those who refuse to get on with Life. The rescuer also gets held back from getting on with his or her own life. Rescuing people from an accident, for example, is a different story, because in this case nobody is trying to deceive you and trap you indefinitely, and these people, when they have recovered sufficiently, carry on getting on with their lives.

It is not possible to rescue people who insist on playing out self negating roles. They will reap negative results. You cannot save them from their folly. However, you can tell them what negative roles they are staging.

Rubbishdump. Another victim role is Rubbishdump, who is the blamed. "I refuse to take responsibility for my actions. I didn't do them [the destructive things I have done]. **You** did them Rubbishdump, not me. I am innocent [deception]." When you catch an ego out with what it is doing and tell it, it very often denies what you say and accuses you of its misdemeanours; or the ego changes the subject and accuses you of having done something terrible, that you have not in fact done, in order to get you caught up in guilt. Then the attention is on you, instead of the nasty things it is doing, so the ego gets away with what it is doing, so it thinks.

Why should you be made to feel awful because someone else "cannot" get his or her life together?

Because the ego is separated from Life it thinks it is exempt from the Law. The Laws are perfect and we get away with nothing. Life is not deceived by any egos. The ego tries to dump its karmic load onto some innocent person, so that it does not have to account for it. In order to play this game it makes out that **you** are the baddy, the culprit, not it and if you fall for this ploy you have been used as a rubbish bin, the receiver of its rubbish.

The ego is the force of separation, death – non-existence – and destruction. It separates you from the truth, the light and reality.

Separation, apartheid, on any level of Life does not work, because it is based on an illusion and is not realistic. Many countries and individuals have used the old South Africa as a rubbishdump and tried to offload their own karma onto the country. If you are still blaming the old South Africa for the separation, apartheid, between your spirit and your personality, the split between your heart and your mind and the racial prejudices of your ego, it will not help you in the least. South Africa is not going to overcome your personal and national problems of the separation for you. The Afrikaners of the old South Africa did not begin **the** separation and racial prejudices on the whole planet. The separation is a global problem that each individual has to address.

"The hell I got myself into [by separating myself from the essential One Life] is your fault Rubbishdump, so I'm going to dump my hell, my ego, onto you."

If the ego does not use you as a rubbish dump it will try another tactic of mind-screwing and tell you that what you have observed about it is **not** what it is doing, and that you don't understand. Exactly what you do not understand, supposedly, is not enlarged on because it is made up nonsense. In this case the ego is trying to blind you to what it is doing.

"I do not want any of my problems Rubbishdump, so let me dump them onto you and blame you for them," say irresponsible people. You do not **have to** take on other people's negative karma and rectify it for them. You did not create it.

Other people's egos require you to sacrifice yourself and your life for them. They want slaves. If you have made a sacrifice of yourself and your life you will not have a life to get on with. You do not **have to** make a sacrifice of yourself.

How to Avoid Getting Trapped by Other Egos

Other people's aggressive egos can trap you with bewildering illusions about yourself, i.e. with false accusations. They judge you, find you guilty, when you are in fact innocent, and hold you captive in prison, **if** you fall for the game. The passive, covert egos trap you with the, "Poor me," game, which may not even be verbalized, and, "If you love me . . . [you'll do exactly what I want you to do for me, and if you don't you're mean and horrible]," game.

These games befuddle one so that one cannot think clearly. Like a spider the ego tangles one up in untrue thoughtforms – spells – which, if accepted as truth, muddle and blind one. This is why it is essential, in any given situation, to bear the truth in mind. The truth is the light and with light we can see clearly.

Both aggressive and passive egos play the, "You owe me," game, in situations where you do not owe them anything. They bribe you emotionally with, "If you do what I want you to do for me, I'll reward you with my love." Then comes the threat and manipulation with fear, "If you do not do what I want you to do for me, I'll reject you, cast you off, and disinherit you," i.e. you deserve to be punished for being "bad".

Egos steal people and their lives by taking possession of them, which means they are cut off from their Source and are no longer free. They possess them in order to use them. You do not **have to** be possessed by others. You are not the possession of someone else's ego, neither do you have the right to possess someone else.

First of all there is no point in **resisting** what other people's egos are doing. "How **dare** John accuse me of this!" The point is that John **has** dared and **is** doing it. So accept that this **is** what is happening. Resistance means that you will or desire the scene to be different, when it is what it is. Accept that John has a free choice, that you have no right to dictate to him or decide what he should or should not do. John, with his free choice, has chosen to play a nasty game with you. However, **you** have a free choice too and John is not your authority, so **you** can decide what happens to you. You do not **have to** accept John's false accusation. Now you can exercise your free choice and say the magic word **"No"**.

"No," means that you are standing up for yourself and putting the ego of another in its place. Resisting an ego and wrestling with it, or being passive and giving into it does not work. Here is a triangle showing how to overcome an ego:—

refusing to play the game
"No, I am not playing this game."
"I do not accept your false accusation.
You can keep it as it is nonsense."
detached
(not participating in the ego's drama)

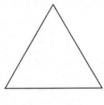

aggressively resisting the game
angry response
"How dare you!"
on the defensive

passive
paralysed by fear
giving in to the game
tiptoeing around an ego, so
you do not upset it, or
running away from it

(trapped in the game
and reacting to the drama)

(trapped in the game
and reacting to the drama)

If you refuse to play the game of the ego you do not have to be caught in it aggressively trying to fight your way out, or passively giving in to it.

No is the most wonderfully liberating word. No, in this context, means:— "No. I do not **have to** accept John's accusation of me. It is not true or fair." "I do not have to be caught in the trap of John's false accusation of me, and get stuck in the prison cell John is offering me."

Before you can say ,"No," with any real conviction, you need to agree with yourself that you are not going to have your quality of life and health destroyed by the ghastly games of any egos, and that you are not going to take their nonsense any more. You have to "put your foot down" and "make a stand" for what you know to be right and just.

The false accusations of the ego are toxic, deadly ideas (illusions) that distort your mind, upset your emotional body and dis-ease your physical body.

No means, "I will not permit you to destroy me with demoralizing insults and false accusations that poison my personality systems to death. I do not accept your false accusations." If you find that you have already accepted an insult or false accusation and it has been disturbing and upsetting you for years, release it and send it back to its creator. You do not **have to** carry it around with you, weighing you down and making your personality sick. The moment you release it you will feel much lighter and the disturbance in your personality is no longer there.

No means, "You are not 'poor' and pathetic. You are quite capable of solving your own problems," i.e. I do not have to fall for your, "Poor me," manipulation.

No means, "No, I do not owe you anything. If I give you anything it is what I choose to give you."

No means, "I refuse to be possessed and held prisoner by you."

No means, "I do not **have to** please your ego, or be victimized by it. I am here to be true to my real self, and do what I know I need to do."

No means that I do not **have to** play the game that some other ego is trying to play with me. For instance, "You are playing the game you-are-the-king-of-the-castle-and-I-have-to-play-the-'guilty'-dirty-rascal, and grovel at your feet and say 'Yes, man'. Well, it is a silly game and I am not going to play it." It takes two to play a game and if one party says, "No. I do not want to play," guess what happens? The game cannot be played. You **can** sabotage the games of other egos.

You do not have to take other people's egos seriously. They are not real. They are ridiculous. The "Poor me" game can be avoided by not playing, "Yes, poor you." The ego may then play another game by accusing you of not loving it, but once again you can say, "No, I don't have to fall for this." **You** have a say in what you choose to do with your life and your time.

If you allow someone else's ego authority over you then you will most likely believe it and fall for its horrible games. What is necessary is that you take 100 per cent responsibility for yourself, be your own authority and be truthful. The truth is the light. Illusions are dark, black thoughtforms. Darkness is dispelled with light.

The truth is that you are **not guilty** of the false accusations and judgements of the ego, so it has no right to hold you prisoner. The ego cannot set anyone free because it is possessive, it cannot forgive because it cannot love and it wants to keep you so that it can use you. Do not wait for ever for some ego to forgive you and let go of you. **You** have to free yourself.

No means, "I do not have to play Atlas and carry you because you refuse to take responsibility for yourself and your life." "I do not have to carry your karma and work it out for you. That is **your** homework."

"No," needs to be said firmly and without aggression. If you become aggressive you may scare the other person, who in turn will become aggressive back. This means that an argument may develop. This is not an argument. You are making a statement.

The ego is a liar. If you are truthful it can't catch you. Speak the truth. For example, "You are talking nonsense!" Shout the truth out, if it is appropriate, or you can keep silent and acknowledge the truth within. Silence is another way to deal with an ego, i.e. there is no response from you, which thwarts the ego's game. This silence is not the stony, seething silence of anger. It is the silence of an audience watching the drama unfolding and doing nothing. In this case the ego cannot do anything with you, because you are not participating in the drama.

If you do get angry use your anger to shout out the truth, the facts, without judging the other person. For example, "You are dumping your psychological rubbish onto me. You can take it right back and take responsibility for it." If you have lost your temper then you know that the other person's ego has got at you in some way. Take a little time for yourself to find out what was said, or what the ego has done. Work through it, release the nasty thing the ego said, etc. If you do this properly you will find that you are no longer angry and have restored your equilibrium.

Every person is unique and their egos play different games. You need to see how each one operates and to be in the moment to find out what works. You do need to work out strategies for each individual ego. Whatever you do, do not give in to other people's egos. This is what they want – for you to give in to them – so that they can get their way.

Who said that you **have to** give into other people's egos and allow them to victimize you? The games of the ego are highly destructive and cause chaos, distress, disease and death. It is necessary to either ignore the games and not play them, i.e. not play the victim, or destroy them.

You do not **have to** sacrifice the truth, reality, Life, your real self, your self-respect or your freedom for any egos and get stuck in hell. You do not **have to** deny your true self and play out some painful victim character role, in hell, that some ego has accused you of "being", when it's a lie.

If you give in to any egos you have lost everything – Life. The ego is a twisted idea about reality, a denial of the truth, reality. It therefore says, "No," to reality, Life, so it is necessary to learn to say, "No," to the ego. If you do not, you become its victim.

No means, "I am not here to be manipulated, used and abused by any egos." **Who** said that you **have to** be used and abused? If you have self-respect you will not allow any egos to abuse you. Of course, if you have an ego you will not have self-respect.

No means, "You are not God. God is my authority. God Knows. You do not know what is best for me, even if you pretend to be the light, so that you can be my authority and order me about. You are not my authority, so therefore you cannot dictate to me, manipulate me and abuse me, as I am not open to you and your nonsense. As I am not open to you, you cannot victimize me."

The ego wants your submission so that it can rule you and do what it wants with you, irrespective of your **needs**. It wants everything to go its way and its way only. When you say, "No," to an ego it will more than likely get angry because it can no longer manipulate you and use you. It may then come out with a tirade of poisonous false accusations and try to make you feel extremely guilty. You have to be strict with it and demonstrate to it over and over again, if necessary, that you will not be taken in and give in to its unfair, if not inhuman, demands.

You do not **have to** do anything another person's ego tells you to do. If an ego declares war on you for refusing to submit to its will you can ignore it and refuse to play out a war game. Obviously if it declares physical war you will have to defend your territory.

Giving into another person's ego does not in any way help the person concerned. You have indulged an ego and allowed it to continue to be disruptive and destructive, and it will continue to treat you with complete disrespect. Giving in also ruins your life. Here we have an all lose situation.

You will find that when you make a stand for the truth and your real self the egocentric person, even after fighting back, treats you with more respect. You have demanded the other person's respect.

If you love your real self and know your true identity and have sincere good will towards others you will be protected from the onslaughts of other egos.

HOW TO BREAK OUT OF PRISON

You need to find out what illusionary ideas and beliefs you have, that you believe to be the truth, the real. They make up your prison. **You** need to dispel your prison. To do this you have to root out all your illusionary ideas and beliefs, decide not to have them, give them up and replace them with truths. Then you can live in the real world, Heaven.

What kills illusions, the dark, i.e. your ignorance, is the truth, the light. These illusions were planted in your mind as seed thoughts. Because you believed them to be true you nurtured them and they became obnoxious weeds. One gets so tied up in these thoughtforms one cannot see the light. You have to clean them up. Playing Cinderella and sweeping all this muck out is not a glamorous task, but it has to be diligently carried out in order for you to save and free yourself and salvage your life.

Any identification that we make with the form aspect imprisons us. This includes the ego – the identification with some aspect of the personality, or the whole personality – and the identification that we may make with an idea, or thoughtform. These ideas can be numerous and include the false accusations and judgements of others that we fell for and believed. For example, "I **am** a worthless baddy," "I **am** a reject," "I **am** dumb," "I **am** a serious intellectual," "I **am** a male, and I am superior to women." These ideas become roles, images, that we then have to play out – the worthless baddy, the reject, the dumbcluck, the serious intellectual, the macho male, with all the clothes (costumes), scripts and props that are appropriate for the part.

Other parts can be unconscious. For example, you have an alcoholic parent who requires to be taken care of and is verbally abusive. This parent is training you to play the Atlas and rubbishdump roles, without you realising it.

These roles can become habits that we continually play out, until one day we realise that we don't have to play them. We need to find out the idea behind the image, weed the idea out, drop it and decide to play out something else. Breaking down old habits requires constant vigilance. We have to recondition ourselves to behave differently.

Eradicating the ego is not so simple. The only way you can effectively dispel the ego is to head straight for the truth, then you have the opportunity of finding your real self, which is a naturally loving, joyful, beautiful being – a "child" of Life – that never was really separated from all of Life. When you realise that the ego – yours and others – is a false "light", not the truth, not the real, not God within – the only true authority – and not your true identity your hell is dispelled consciously. When you see the light, the truth of what your real identity is your false "self", your ego, and your depressing hell disintegrate. This means that you can give up all your binding ego attachments and its desires. Put the truth **first**, above illusions. The truth is what counts, not illusions. Illusions are totally irrelevant and must be discarded.

When you give up your ego you give up your illusionary separation from Life. You can then come Home to your real self, Life, the real world. You are the real, not an absurd illusion about yourself.

You can only consciously break out of prison when you become aware of who you really are – an aspect of Life Divine – and who you are not; in other words be able to discern the real from the unreal. The inner conflict, war, is between the real and the false "self", the actual and the make-believe. Your true identity gets rid of the false "self", the illusionary separation, feelings of inferiority and fear.

When you discover your true identity – the One Glorious Life, that permeates all of Creation – you are, in conscious awareness, no longer trapped and bound in form in the one specific, limited thoughtform of your ego, and in a host of other miscellaneous thoughtforms that you thought were aspects of your real self. This is when you come Home, back to essential Life, to our Creator or God that made you, and the journey through matter is complete. This is when you realise that your real self is much more than you ever thought, or dreamed, that what you are essentially is a radiant, magnificent, beautiful, God made being, without any flaws. Knowing this you can rejoice in being, in Life. This is when you "fall in love" with Life, with being, with the Creator and the Creation and you feel marvellous and joyful. You have saved yourself and your life.

CHAPTER 7

SERVICE

In reality there is One whole, Glorious Life. We have been given the marvellous gift of life, together with the nature kingdoms, by our God.

In reality there is only the One Life to love, to give to and to serve. If your life is based on the truth, the real then you serve Life. If your life is centred around your avaricious, separated ego and other illusions then you are working against yourself, Life, the real and the creation. This is a **dis**service to the One Life. You cannot work against Life and for Life at the same time.

Although there are an infinite number of ways to serve, the greatest service that you can give this world is to lift your conscious awareness and your personality Up into the light of the truth, to learn to love and to learn wisdom. If each person worked at his or her own salvation this planet would be salvaged.

Once you have brought yourself Up you can bring love and light to the world. You can bring Heaven to Earth.

Physical sex is not the ultimate union. Getting your world together means overcoming the illusion of separation. The at-onement, marriage or union, of the Heaven and Earth aspects – your spirit and your personality – in your conscious awareness and individual world, enables you to bring the light, Heaven, to Earth.

If you let your real self be then you will let this world be too.

Practice **harmlessness** and learn to use your creative abilities constructively. We all have to take responsibility for what we are doing, creating, and for what we are allowing others to do to us.

In order to serve we need to listen deep within to sense what is needed now. The more you give the more you receive. The grabbing ego with its "only me" attitude gives absolutely nothing. If it "gives" anything it is "given" to impress others and to improve its image, which is not a service. Serve because you love and care for all.

Give and share everything that you have to offer to uplift the world. Acknowledge the divinity in all. Give to others what is appropriate for them in the moment, so tune into where people are at. You need to listen to them carefully and be sensitive to their needs. People are equally important, but they have not arrived at equal levels of conscious awareness. Do not try to impose your theories and beliefs onto them and force them to accept them.

You cannot make other people happy. You are not responsible for their choices and actions. You are responsible for your actions. In order to be of service you need to be detached, not involved and caught up in other people's misery.

You cannot prevent suffering. Suffering is the effect. Illusion is the cause, so you need to find the cause of the suffering and rectify that. Having dispelled the illusion – the cause – suffering – the effect – comes to an end.

Do not serve other people's egos. Allowing other people's egos to use and abuse you is not a service. The negative games of the ego bear no fruit; they are a waste.

OUR PLANET

Humanity sorrows for the glorious Life it lost sight of and separated itself from. That which is causing all the misery, distress, deserts, corruption, pollution, waste, wars and purposeless destruction on the planet is mankind's ego. Without this threatening menace and danger we would all live in peace and co-operation. We would share this planet together as one humanity, one family, and work towards the benefit of all of Creation, the Whole. Humanity and the nature kingdoms would flourish and we could co-create with God a new world, a new civilization, in which **the Whole of Creation would succeed**. There is nothing to stop us but humanity's absurd ego.

The ego is extremely expensive and a bad investment. It is a terrible

waste. The human ego is not only wrecking the global economy it is also wrecking and crucifying you and the planet and turning it into a wasteland.

If you want to clean up the planet and save, heal and free it, save, heal and free yourself and your life. It is quite simple – if you do not get rid of your untrue, sickening ideas, including your ego, they are going to kill your personality and the planet. The planet and God's Plan matter.

Sacrifice means giving up illusion for the real, death (non-existence, i.e. illusion) for Life. Since the real is bliss and gives you joy, happiness, contentment, satisfaction and fullness, giving up impoverishing illusion is no great sacrifice.

You have to sacrifice Life, Reality, your true self in order to live in hell with your ego. In order to get back to Life, reality, your self you have to sacrifice your dead – non-existent – ego.

Every time you surmount a difficulty and find some light you bring more light into your world and the planet. You lighten the vibrations of humanity, so you can and you are perfectly capable of making a significant and worthwhile difference to the Whole.

In reality we are not separate from God's Plan and Purpose. We do not have to do anything about the way God created this world. We need to find out what really Is and work with God's Purpose for this Creation.

Essentially everything in Life is in perfect order. Our lives are inherently perfectly beautiful. Why wastefully throw this away for our foolish egos? In a spirit of co-operation, good will, love and respect for all of Life – each other and the nature kingdoms – we can co-create with God within Heaven on Earth. We can allow Earth to be the paradise She Is and so live in it joyfully and happily **together**. This is a golden opportunity that we have now. It is up to us. We have to choose to do it and we can find the way to do it, so let us get on with working towards it. What are we waiting for?

INDEX

YOUR INNER JOURNEY TO THE REAL